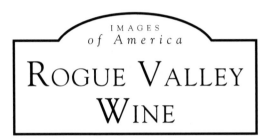

IMAGES
of America

ROGUE VALLEY WINE

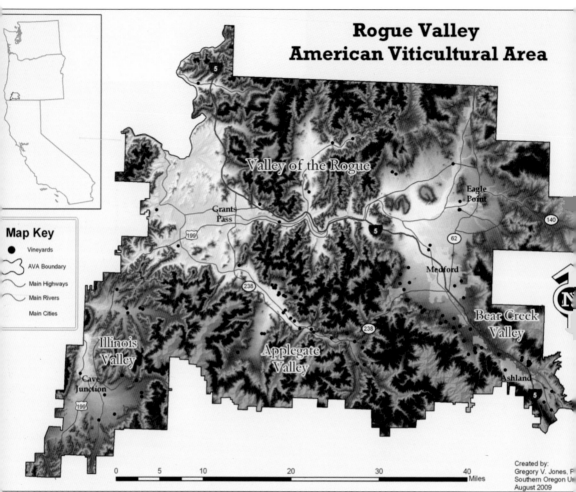

Rogue Valley
American Viticultural Area

Valley of the Rogue

Eagle
Point

Grants
Pass

Medford

Bear Creek
Valley

Illinois
Valley

Applegate
Valley

Cave
Junction

Ashland

N

Map Key

● Vineyards

〰 AVA Boundary

〰 Main Highways

〰 Main Rivers

Main Cities

0   5   10   20   30   40
                                          Miles

Created by:
Gregory V. Jones, P
Southern Oregon Un
August 2009

Oregon's Rogue Valley American Viticultural Area (AVA) lies just north of the California border. The Applegate Valley AVA lies entirely within the Rogue Valley AVA. Two other winegrowing regions not yet recognized by the Federal Bureau of Alcohol, Tobacco, and Firearms are the Illinois Valley and the Bear Creek Valley. Vineyard locations appear as dots. (Courtesy of Prof. Gregory V. Jones of Southern Oregon University.)

IMAGES
of America

ROGUE VALLEY
WINE

MJ Daspit and Eric Weisinger

ARCADIA
PUBLISHING

Published by Arcadia Publishing
Charleston, South Carolina

Printed in the United States of America

Library of Congress Control Number: 2010926988

For all general information, please contact Arcadia Publishing:
Telephone 843-853-2070
Fax 843-853-0044
E-mail sales@arcadiapublishing.com
For customer service and orders:
Toll-Free 1-888-313-2665

Visit us on the Internet at www.arcadiapublishing.com

*This book is dedicated to the growers and vintners who
created the wine industry of the Rogue Valley.*

CONTENTS

Acknowledgments   6

Introduction   7

1.   The 1850s through Prohibition   9

2.   The Revival and Today's Wine Scene   17

3.   Individuals Who Have Influenced the Industry   93

4.   Tasting Venues and Events   101

Bibliography   126

Index   127

ACKNOWLEDGMENTS

All of the vineyard and winery owners featured in *Rogue Valley Wine* have contributed their photographs, stories, and time to the making of this book. Few businesses require the commitment of time and capital that wine grape growing and winemaking do. From planting vines and bringing in the harvest to making the wine and marketing, this industry demands a variety of skills unlike any other. It would be, one winemaker said, like a baker having to grow the wheat, mill it, bake the bread, package it, and then sell it.

Columnist Cleve Twitchell, who writes on wine for Medford's *Mail Tribune*, contributed much information, as did winemaker and historian Dr. Willard Brown, whose time line of wine industry development in the Rogue Valley appears on the Rogue Valley Winegrowers Association Web site. Prof. Porter Lombard provided information on viticultural research conducted at the Oregon State University (OSU) Southern Oregon Experiment Station at Hanley Road. Prof. Gregory V. Jones of Southern Oregon University provided technical information and the graphic image illustrating the location, topography, and vineyard locations in the Rogue Valley AVA. Adam L. Miller, architect with OgdenRoemerWilkerson, contributed maps of winery locations. Margaret LaPlante culled the Southern Oregon Historical Society's photograph and print archives for information on Rogue Valley winemaking from the 1850s through Prohibition. Cricket Hill Vineyard owner and winemaker Duane Bowman, by virtue of his position on the Board of Directors of the Rogue Valley Winegrowers Association and the Applegate Valley Vintners Association, helped with contacting vineyard and winery owners throughout the region and garnered support for our project. Rogue Valley photographers Steve Addington of Kiaterna Design Group, Orville Hector of Orville's Photography, Laurie Passey of Laurie Passey Photography, Michael D. Davis of Heart to Art–Studio D Photography, Michelle Binker of the *Illinois Valley News*, Ed Dunsavage, and Teena Jo contributed images. Larry Landis, OSU archivist, granted permission for use of OSU images. Robert Hunter, editor at the Medford *Mail Tribune*, granted permission for use of *Mail Tribune* images.

Unless otherwise noted, photographs appear courtesy of the authors.

INTRODUCTION

Southern Oregon's Rogue Valley lies between the Siskiyou Mountains and the Cascade Range, an area drained by the Illinois River, the Applegate River, and Bear Creek—all tributaries of the Rogue River, which empties into the Pacific Ocean. This watershed roughly defines the Rogue Valley American Viticultural Area (AVA), officially recognized by the Federal Bureau of Alcohol, Tobacco, and Firearms (BATF) in 1991 as the most southerly of 16 Oregon AVAs. In 2000, the Applegate Valley was recognized as a distinct AVA lying entirely within the Rogue Valley AVA.

The great diversity of climate, topography, and soils in the Rogue Valley supports cultivation of warm- and cool-climate grape varieties. The most recent (2009) U.S. Department of Agriculture Oregon Vineyard and Winery Report shows 1,984 acres planted to wine grapes in the Rogue Valley AVA. Of the reds, the variety with the largest total acreage planted is Pinot Noir, followed by Syrah, Merlot, and Cabernet Sauvignon. Of the whites, Pinot Gris, Chardonnay, White Riesling, and Gewürztraminer predominate. The Rogue Valley Winegrowers Association reports significant acreage also planted to Tempranillo, Malbec, Cabernet Franc, and Viognier. In 2008 and 2009, the largest total tonnage of one variety crushed by Rogue Valley wineries was Pinot Noir, followed by Pinot Gris, Merlot, White Riesling, Syrah, Cabernet Sauvignon, Chardonnay, Viognier, and Gewürztraminer.

The very first vineyards in Oregon were planted over 150 years ago in the Rogue Valley. Jacksonville's Peter Britt is credited with testing over 200 types of grapes for suitability to Rogue Valley conditions, including varieties from Bordeaux, Burgundy, Alsace, Germany, and North America. Though newspapers of the time made much of the market for Rogue Valley table grapes, articles also allude to wine made from the surplus crop.

As early as 1887, Jacksonville's *Democratic Times* expressed strong objections to a proposed state prohibition amendment that would stifle a vibrant vineyard industry. By 1890, the Oregon State Board of Agriculture reported over 100 acres planted to grapes by more than a dozen growers in the Jacksonville area. It noted that Col. J. N. T. Miller of Jacksonville, thought to be the state's largest grower, used half of his 20-acre harvest for making wine, while Peter Britt crushed the entire harvest of his 5 acres.

Prohibition was declared law in Oregon in 1916. By 1933, when repeal took effect nationally, Rogue Valley viticulture had been eclipsed by cultivation of tree fruit (especially pears) and berries. It was not until the late 1960s, with the establishment of the experimental vineyard at the OSU Southern Oregon Experiment Station, that interest in wine grape production in the Rogue Valley revived.

By this time, pioneering wine grape growers—primarily interested in producing Pinot Noir—were establishing vineyards in the Willamette Valley and Umpqua Valley to the north. It was not until the early 1970s that the first wave of winegrowers established vineyards in the Rogue Valley. By 1987, the first year statistics were collected by the state for the Rogue Valley, 38 vineyards totaling 302 acres were planted to wine grapes, and five wineries crushed 514 tons of grapes.

The 2009 Oregon Vineyard and Winery Report puts the number of Rogue Valley vineyards at 113, total acreage planted at 1,984, and production at 4,935 tons. Forty-two wineries reportedly crushed 2,719 tons.

Still, in spite of rapid growth in the 20-some years for which we have statistics, the Rogue Valley remains largely undiscovered. It is common for visitors to remark that the Rogue Valley today, with its off-the-beaten-path boutique wineries, is like the Napa Valley of the 1970s. While the trend in winemaking is toward growing sophistication and refinement, most winemakers themselves remain accessible, often on hand in tasting rooms pouring for visitors. Perhaps because the region has yet to experience wide notoriety, this volume is the only book to date—apart from academic studies—to focus exclusively on the wine industry of the Rogue Valley.

Rogue Valley Wine is intended not only as a historical review but also as a guide that may be used by readers interested in visiting the wineries and attending the events described. The chapter on modern wineries discusses three naturally distinct geographical areas within the Rogue Valley AVA: the area that surrounds Oregon Highway 199 from Cave Junction to Grants Pass, known as the Illinois Valley; the area west of Jacksonville along Oregon Highway 238, recognized as the Applegate Valley AVA; and the area along the Interstate 5 corridor (including the Bear Creek Valley) running from Ashland to Grants Pass. A map showing principal roads and winery locations is provided for each of these areas. For clarity, the terms "winery," "vineyard," "cellars," and so forth have been omitted from map locations except where confusion with a geographical feature, such as Crater Lake, would result.

Although most winemakers will say that good wine is grown rather than made, it was impossible to include information on all of the Rogue Valley's 113 vineyards. Apart from vineyards associated with wineries, only those with historical significance have been specifically mentioned in this volume. Likewise, due to space limitations, most virtual wineries have not been included. By a virtual winery, we mean a venture that produces a commercial label without necessarily being affiliated with a vineyard or a winery. By buying grapes and making wine through a "custom crush" arrangement with a winery (which affords use of facilities and can include the services of the resident winemaker), anyone can—upon state approval of a label—produce commercial vintages. With the advent of the Rogue Valley's first exclusively custom crush facility, Pallet Wine Company in Medford, the trend toward the virtual winery is expected to ramp up.

While this book is a history going back to the origins of the Rogue Valley wine industry, it is also a snapshot of wine grape growing and winemaking as of 2010. Such is the vigor of the industry that we fully expect the number of vineyards and wineries on record as of this writing will have grown by the time of publication. We applaud those who will have emerged in the interim and regret their omission.

One

THE 1850S THROUGH PROHIBITION

Lured by gold, Swiss immigrant Peter Britt arrived in Jacksonville in 1852. He built a cabin on a hillside at the edge of town and took up mule skinning, supplying miners with food and tools that he packed in from Crescent City, California. By 1856, he had made enough money to devote his time to a variety of other pursuits: photography, horticulture, meteorology, beekeeping, and making wine.

Britt's vineyard is thought to have occupied the hillside where music lovers now spread their blankets to enjoy summer concerts presented by Jacksonville's Britt Festivals. Britt obtained his cuttings of mission grapes from California in 1854 but eventually planted many varieties of *Vitis vinifera*. As his viticultural experiments grew, he expanded to a vineyard site about a mile outside of town. Rogue Valley viticultural historian Dr. Willard Brown has written that Britt grew Cabernet Sauvignon, Zinfandel, Riesling, Malbec, Petite Sirah, Semillon, Sauvignon Blanc, Merlot, Cabernet Franc, Traminer, and possibly the first Pinot Noir in Oregon.

Britt supplied cuttings to others, and by 1890, there were over 40 acres of vines in the Jacksonville area. The quality of grapes produced by Col. J. N. T. Miller, Amile Barbe, Raphael Morat, and August Petard was frequently reported in Jacksonville's *Democratic Times* and the *Oregon Sentinel*. The newspapers also reported activities of local temperance societies. The November 4, 1887, edition of the *Democratic Times* reported on local grape growing, observing that "with the completion of the O & C road to California a market will be opened and the acreage in vineyards and orchards will be rapidly increased. At present the pending prohibition amendment has deterred large numbers from setting out vineyards. A German, representing a colony, had determined to purchase 10,000 acres of land in the valley, with the idea of converting it into a vineyard; but when he learned of the prohibition amendment concluded that until the election was over he would not invest." The prohibition amendment on the state ballot that year did not pass but would in 1914. Taking effect in Oregon in 1916, prohibition dismantled the wine industry.

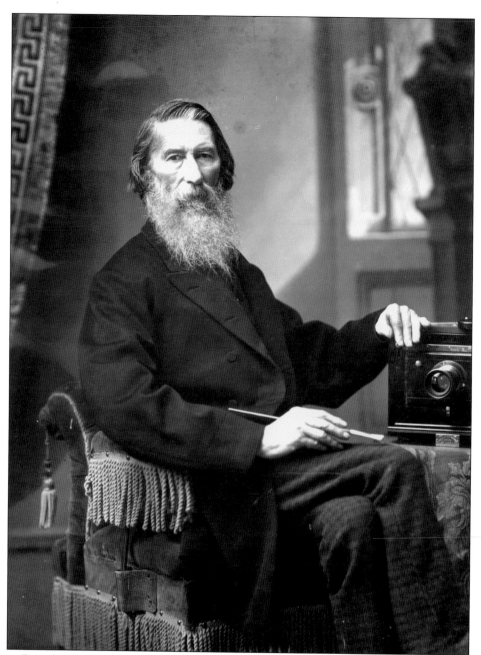

Peter Britt (1819–1905) is credited with establishing Oregon's first vineyard in the mid-1850s. In 1858, Britt became the first person to produce wine in the Oregon Territory. In 1873, he was informed by the Internal Revenue Service that he owed taxes on the wine he had sold. He settled the issue, which involved getting a business license, and named his commercial enterprise Valley View Vineyard. Britt sold most of the wine produced by his vineyard to neighbors but also shipped his product by stagecoach and railroad to other regions. The vintages produced by Britt and his fellow Jacksonville-area winemakers were often reviewed favorably when compared to California wines, the benchmark of excellence at the time. (SOHS #725, courtesy of the Southern Oregon Historical Society.)

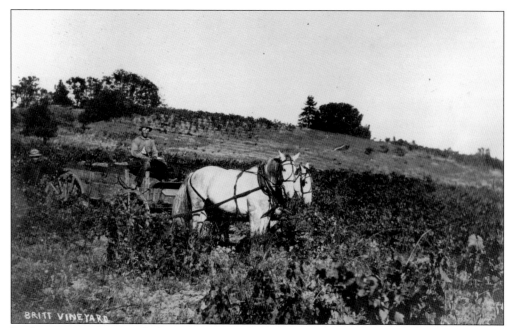

By the time Peter Britt took this picture around 1880, his vineyard property had grown to 15 acres, and Valley View Vineyard was producing 1,000 to 3,000 gallons of wine per year, which he sold locally for 50¢ a gallon. (SOHS #4534, courtesy of the Southern Oregon Historical Society.)

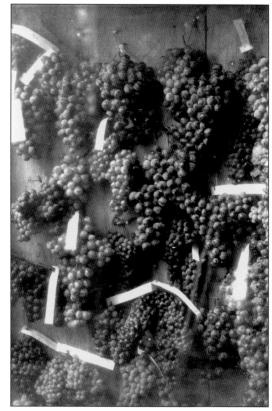

Peter Britt introduced over 200 grape varieties to Oregon. On October 1, 1889, the *Democratic Times* reported, "Emil Britt [Peter's son] yesterday favored us with a huge basket of specimen bunches from the Britt vineyard of surpassing excellence, consisting of Mission, Rose of Peru, Purple Chasselas, Black Malvoisie, Isabella, and Salem varieties." (SOHS #1902, courtesy of the Southern Oregon Historical Society.)

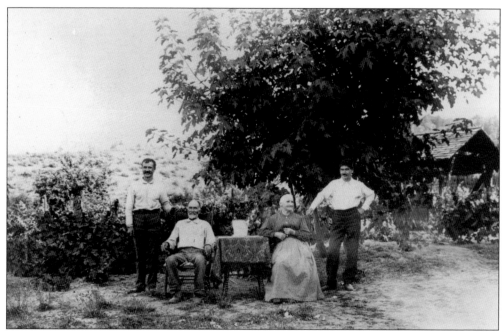

The August Petard family, shown above picnicking, also cultivated grapes in Jacksonville. Their vineyard, below, exemplifies early viticultural techniques, such as head pruning. One A. H. Carson of Josephine County lectured the Farmer's Institute in Ashland on proper methods of grape culture. On November 28, 1889, the *Democratic Times* reported that he began by stating, "It would be useless to say we cannot grow grapes in Southern Oregon as anyone visiting the small vineyards in Josephine and Jackson counties will be convinced that this is the home of the grape as far as soil and climate are concerned. The only thing we lack here is the knowledge as to the varieties and to the proper method of cultivation and pruning, and, I might add, the energy and go-ahead to put that knowledge into practical shape." (SOHS #4498 and #4496, both courtesy of the Southern Oregon Historical Society.)

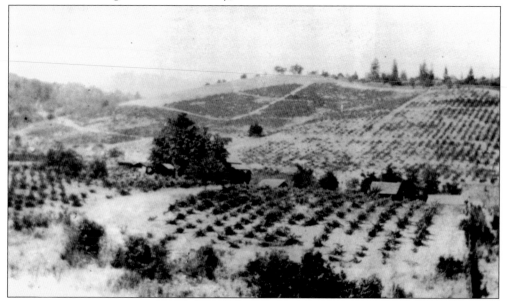

Col. J. N. T. Miller owned a 16-acre Jacksonville vineyard, producing 50 tons of grapes annually. On November 4, 1887, the *Democratic Times* envisioned widespread production on this scale: "Within the next few years much of the Rogue River valley will be exclusively devoted to viticulture. The climate and soil are such that grapes of all varieties flourish there and attain the greatest perfection." (Unnumbered, courtesy of the Southern Oregon Historical Society.)

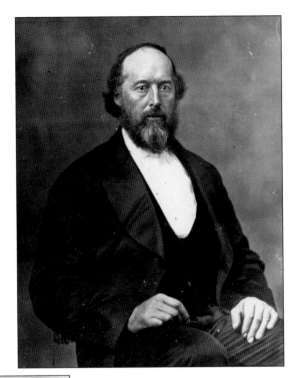

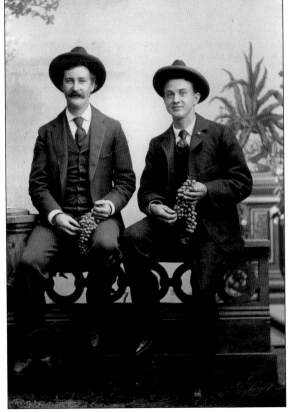

Emil Britt (left) and John Miller, son of Col. J. N. T. Miller, pose with grapes from Peter Britt's vineyard. Both Peter Britt and Colonel Miller sent boxes of grapes to the *Democratic Times* and the *Oregon Sentinel*. These early public relations efforts elicited print testimonial as to the beauty and flavor of their fruit. (SOHS #11735, courtesy of the Southern Oregon Historical Society.)

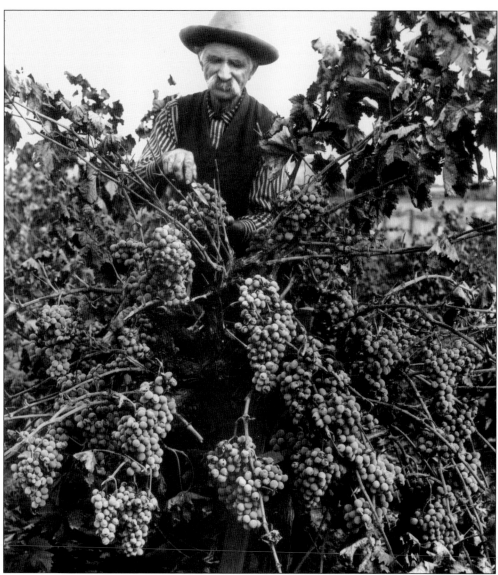

Through the early years of the 20th century, Rogue Valley viticulture continued to flourish. A story on yields of Jacksonville vineyards appearing in the *Ashland Tidings* of December 20, 1889, reported that Peter Britt's harvest from 3 acres of grapes made 1,000 gallons of wine that year. Raphael Morat's 10 acres of vines yielded 1,700 gallons of wine and 200 gallons of brandy. Emil Barbe's 6-acre vineyard produced 1,200 gallons of wine, and J. N. T. Miller's 16 acres of vines produced 800 gallons of wine. The article notes that Morat and Miller shipped the balance of their crops to Portland for sale as fresh fruit. The report calculated the net profit per acre from vineyard land in Jackson County at $75, opining, "This should certainly be sufficient inducement to quadruple the acreage in grapes the coming season. Raisin grapes are among the varieties already growing, and no doubt we could engage as successfully in making raisins as wine." (SOHS #12777, courtesy of the Southern Oregon Historical Society.)

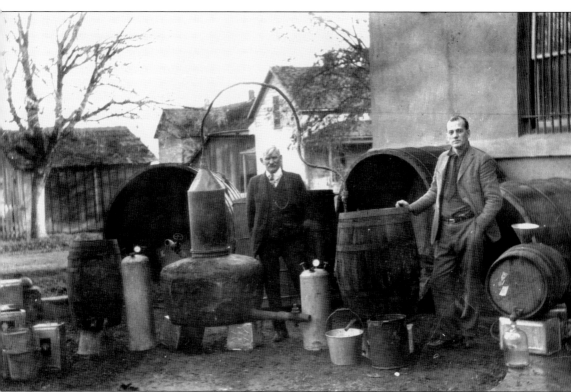

After many years of work, starting with the formation of the Oregon Temperance Society by Methodist missionaries in the Willamette Valley in 1836, antialcohol forces succeeded in enacting prohibition in Oregon in 1914. The Enforcement Act passed by the Oregon legislature banned manufacture and sale of liquor, as well as accepting orders for liquor, printing ads for liquor, and giving away liquor. Doctors were permitted to prescribe and drugstores to carry it for sale by prescription, and a person could bring up to 5 gallons of wine and spirits and up to 20 gallons of beer per month into the state. The Oregon law took effect four years before the ban on alcohol went into effect nationwide in 1920. Outside the Jacksonville jail around the early 1920s, lawmen Charlie Terrell (left) and L. D. Farncrooh display confiscated liquor and winemaking equipment. (SOHS #7891, courtesy of the Southern Oregon Historical Society.)

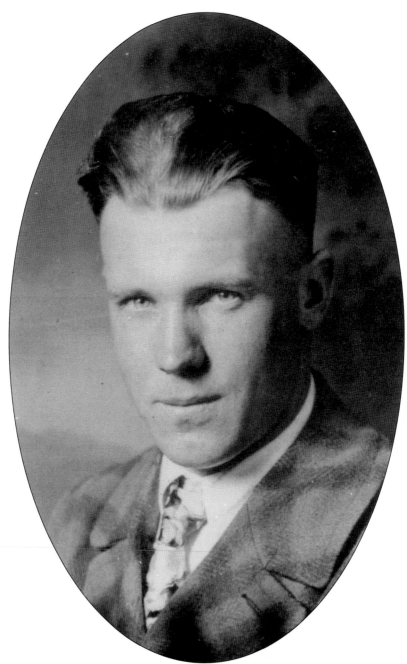

Twenty-five-year-old Ashland police officer Sam Prescott, eulogized in the *Ashland Daily Tidings* (January 24, 1931) as "the Nemisis of rum-runners," was shot and killed in Ashland by presumed bootlegger James C. Adams (also known as James C. Kingsley) on January 24, 1931. Prescott stopped the stolen DeSoto sedan Adams was driving along Main Street in Ashland. When Prescott approached and asked for the driver's identification, Adams shot the officer three times. Adams fled but was apprehended less than two hours after the incident, which turned out to be unrelated to liquor dealing. Having confessed to the murder, Adams was hanged in Salem, Oregon, before 75 witnesses. (SOHS #2045, courtesy of the Southern Oregon Historical Society.)

Two

THE REVIVAL AND TODAY'S WINE SCENE

After the repeal of Prohibition in 1933, there was little interest in commercial grape growing in the Rogue Valley until 1967, when horticulturalist Porter Lombard planted an experimental vineyard at the OSU Experiment Station in Central Point. Lombard found Chenin Blanc, Gewürztraminer, Muscat Blanc, Sauvignon Blanc, Cabernet Sauvignon, and Pinot Noir thrived in the Rogue Valley. Viticultural historian Dr. Willard Brown notes that Lombard's work had a profound influence on the development of the industry in that he provided prospective growers "both grape cuttings and sage advice."

After attending a 1972 Rogue Community College course in viticulture conceived by Dick Troon, Frank Wisnovsky, Roger and Barrie Layne, and Troon established the first vineyards in the Applegate Valley. Dunbar Carpenter and John Ousterhout put in the earliest vineyards near Medford. In the Illinois Valley, Ted Gerber and Suzi and Chuck David were the first commercial growers.

In 1978, Frank Wisnovsky's Valley View Winery and Suzi David's Siskiyou Winery were bonded. By 1986, two new wineries had sprung up in the Illinois Valley: Bridgeview and Foris. In Ashland two years later, Ashland Vineyards and Weisinger's of Ashland opened wineries. The Rogue Valley began to develop its own character as a wine region and was recognized in 1991 as a distinct AVA within the Southern Oregon AVA.

By 1997, there were 51 vineyards and 10 wineries operating in the Rogue Valley. That same year, climatologist Gregory V. Jones began work at Ashland's Southern Oregon University. His studies of Rogue Valley climate and soils began to impact the grape varieties under cultivation. Jones's earlier work in Bordeaux, France, led him to conclude that certain areas of the Rogue Valley were better suited to Bordeaux varieties than Burgundian and Alsatian varieties. At the OSU experimental vineyard, warm-weather varieties—such as Tempranillo, Viognier, Syrah, Nebbiolo, Cabernet Franc, and Merlot—had been under cultivation since 1989. Increasingly, growers tailored their selection of grape varieties to very specific site conditions. With establishment of the Applegate Valley AVA in 2000, such distinctions within the Rogue Valley were officially recognized.

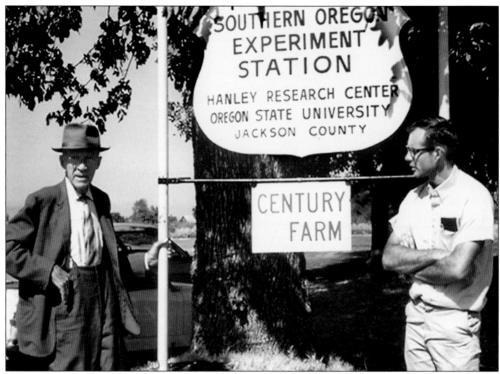

Established in 1911, the Southern Oregon Experiment Station at 569 Hanley Road, Central Point, was chartered to study the effects of local soils and climate on agriculture. It was largely devoted to pear research when Prof. Porter Lombard became superintendent. Retired superintendent F. C. Reimer (left) appears with Lombard in 1967, the year Lombard planted Pinot Noir, Chardonnay, Cabernet Sauvignon, Grenache, Zinfandel, and Muscat Blanc. (Photograph by Robert W. Henderson, courtesy of OSU.)

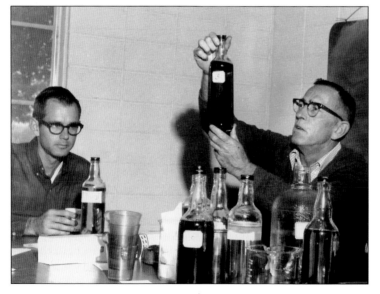

Prof. Porter Lombard (left) and Don Root of Sobroso Fruit Concentrate Company taste flavored pear wine made by Dr. Hoya Yang of OSU in 1968. Jackson County Extension agent Cliff Cordy was skeptical of efforts to produce quality wine grapes in the Rogue Valley since, as he put it, "I grew up in Napa Valley and this is no Napa Valley." (Courtesy of Prof. Porter Lombard.)

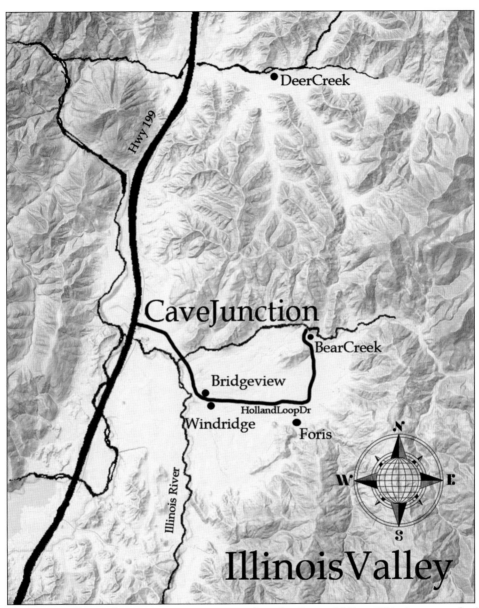

The Illinois Valley is the westernmost region within the Rogue Valley AVA. It surrounds the town of Cave Junction and follows the course of the Illinois River and its tributaries through the Siskiyou and Klamath Mountains. The Illinois Valley is distinctly cooler and wetter than other Rogue Valley growing areas. Average vineyard elevation is 1,474 feet. Precipitation through most of the region averages 55 to 75 inches annually. These conditions make the Illinois Valley a prime growing site for Pinot Noir, Chardonnay, Gewürztraminer, Riesling, Pinot Gris, Pinot Blanc, Early Muscat, and Gamay Noir. A 2001 study of the Rogue Valley by Prof. Gregory V. Jones puts the acreage planted to Pinot Noir at over 50 percent of total vineyard acreage. Shown on the map are wineries operating in the region today. A winery at Rogue River Vineyards opened in 1988 but passed from the scene. Siskiyou Vineyards Winery, established in 1978, was acquired by Bridgeview in 1996 and renamed Bear Creek. (Map by Adam L. Miller, courtesy of OgdenRoemerWilkerson Architecture.)

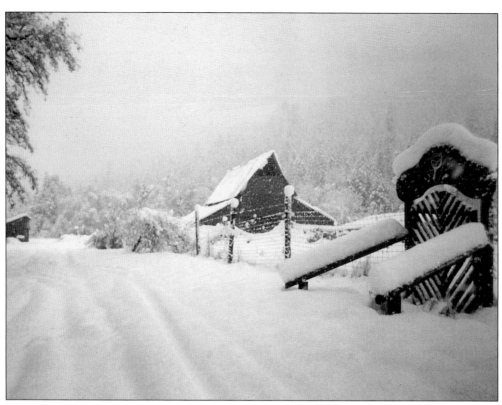

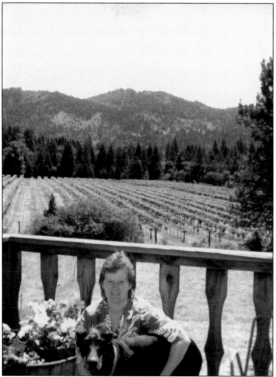

Planted in 1974, Siskiyou Vineyards, shown here in snow, was conceived when Chuck and Suzi (C. J.) David decided to buy John Seidler's Bear Creek Ranch in the Cave Junction area of the Illinois Valley. Seidler, a horticulturalist, showed the Davids the *Vitis vinifera* plants that he had been experimenting with. The Davids planted the first 6 acres of their vineyard the following spring. (Courtesy of C. J. David.)

Siskiyou Vineyards Winery was bonded in 1978. First vintages were estate Cabernet Sauvignon, Pinot Noir, and Gewürztraminer made by Bill Nelson and Dave Anderson of Eugene. *Grants Pass Courier* reporter Donna Devine, left, did a story on the business and became enthralled with the idea of making wine. Schooled by Nelson and Anderson, Devine served as winemaker at Siskiyou Vineyards before moving on to Weisinger's and Troon. (Courtesy of C. J. David.)

This 1982 Siskiyou Vineyards label bears the designation "BW-OR-72," meaning Siskiyou was licensee number 72 among bonded beer and wine producers in Oregon. The notation was subsequently dropped, probably when Federal BATF labeling laws were updated in 1986. (Courtesy of C. J. David.)

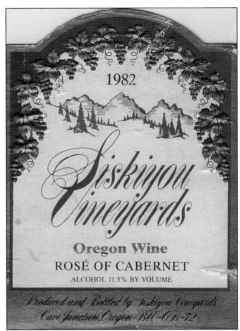

In this photograph from a 1988 Medford *Mail Tribune* article on Rogue Valley wineries by Cleve Twitchell, Suzi David (right) and daughter Kristen label bottles by hand. At its peak, the winery produced 5,000 to 7,000 cases a year. Besides estate Cabernet Sauvignon, Pinot Noir, and Gewürztraminer, Siskiyou produced Chardonnay, Sauvignon Blanc, Riesling, Early Muscat, Zinfandel, and Merlot sourced from other Southern Oregon vineyards. (Courtesy of the *Mail Tribune*.)

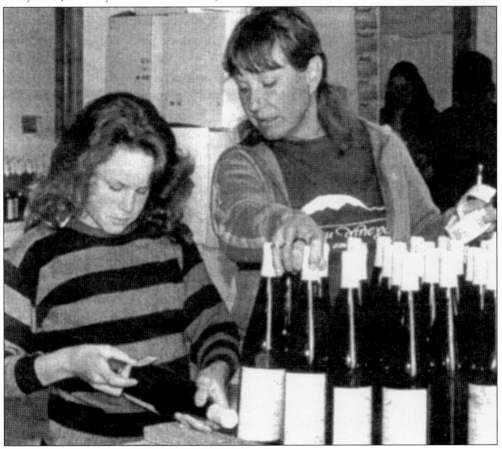

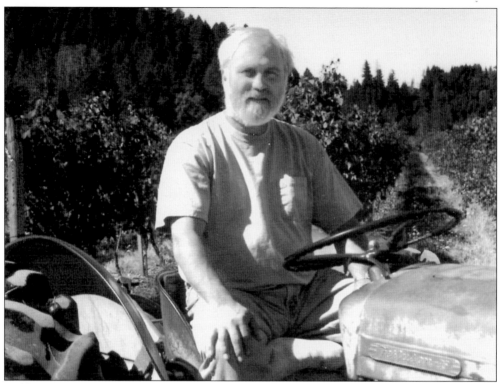

Ted Gerber acquired hillside acreage in the Illinois Valley with a vineyard in mind in 1971. Having collected climate data on his acreage—only 7 miles north of the California border and 25 miles due east of the Pacific Ocean—and having worked with OSU on experimental plantings, Gerber established Foris Vineyards with Alsatian and Burgundy varieties in 1975. Below, Gerber is shown in 1976 on a tractor used to farm his then 4-acre vineyard. Above is Gerber on the same tractor in 2008. By that time, his vineyards had grown to 114 acres planted to Chardonnay, Pinot Gris, Pinot Blanc, Gewürztraminer, Riesling, Early Muscat, and seven Dijon clones of Pinot Noir. Besides producing 80 percent of the grapes used to make Foris wines, Gerber's vineyard supplies grafting stock to top California wineries. (Both, courtesy of Foris Winery and Vineyards.)

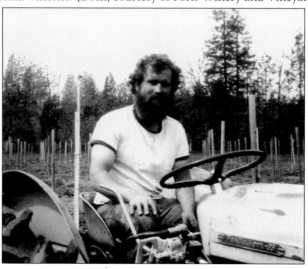

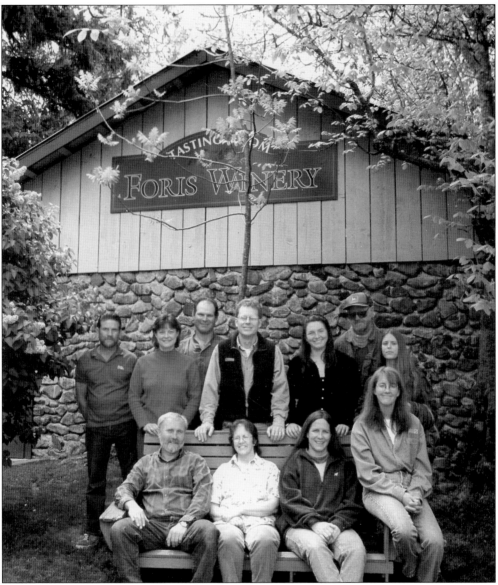

Foris grapes were contracted to vintners throughout Southern Oregon until establishment of the estate winery in 1986. Winery staff of the 1990s included, from left to right, (first row) Ted Gerber, Meri Gerber, Julianne Allen, and Sarah Powell; (second row) Sam Ewing, Dena Trinity, Doyne Podhorsky, Pat Burns, Heather Keribal, George Sickler, and Cere Stetson. Winemaker Sarah Powell joined Foris in 1990. She worked with Gerber to develop a house style based on low vineyard yields (3 tons per acre or less) and minimal manipulation in the winery, resulting in intense, fruit-driven vintages. Gerber eschews competitions, but one benchmark of his wine's excellence is that Foris 1994 Maple Ranch Pinot Noir was selected to be served at a 1997 White House dinner. After Sarah Powell left Foris in 2001, Michael McAuley and Steve Harrington made the wine until Bryan Wilson became winemaker in 2007. Annual production has grown to 54,000 cases, but the winemaking style has remained the same, with an emphasis on growing the quality in the vineyard and an absence of glitz. (Courtesy of Foris Winery and Vineyards.)

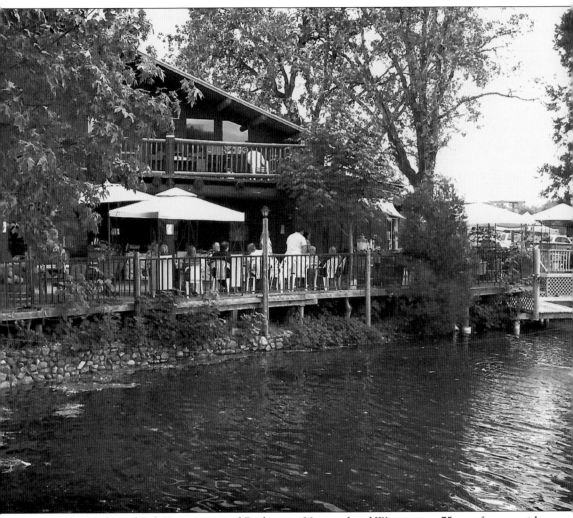

In 1986, Lelo and Bob Kerivan started Bridgeview Vineyard and Winery on a 75-acre farm outside Cave Junction. They put in Chardonnay, Pinot Noir, Pinot Gris, Riesling, and Gewürztraminer in rows only 6 feet apart, keeping 20 buds per vine—which is consistent with European practice. Their unconventional techniques raised eyebrows, but today Bridgeview ranks as one of the largest wineries in Oregon, with production capacity of 100,000 cases per year and sales in 43 states. Bridgeview's most popular product is Blue Moon Riesling, an off-dry white bottled in blue glass that represents over half of the winery's total sales. The Bridgeview Vineyards winery and tasting room stands on a pond amid lush woods typical of the Cave Junction area. Thousands of visitors are drawn to the winery each year, due in part to nearby attractions, such as Oregon Caves. (Photograph by Michelle Binker, courtesy of the *Illinois Valley News*.)

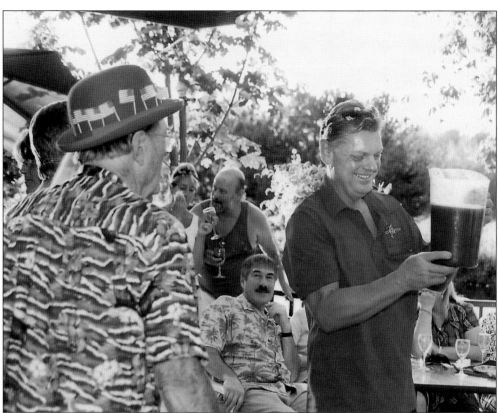

Lelo Kerivan's son René Eichmann (right) holds a pitcher of juice produced at Bridgeview's annual grape stomp. Eichmann became winemaker in 1980. With the acquisition of Siskiyou Vineyards (renamed Bear Creek) and 80 acres in the Applegate Valley, Eichmann produces a broad range of wines, including Bordeaux and Rhone varietals using estate fruit almost exclusively. (Photograph by Michelle Binker, courtesy of the *Illinois Valley News*.)

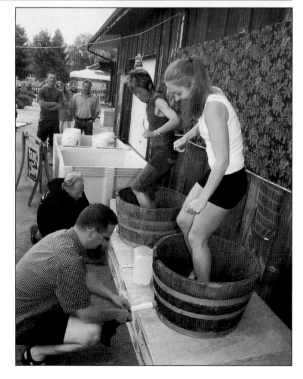

Bridgeview's large winery deck is a perfect site for celebrations, including the annual grape stomp, a tradition since 2007. Here, unidentified grape stomp participants try to produce enough juice to fill the quarter-moon cobalt blue bottle that has become the symbol of Bridgeview's Blue Moon Riesling. (Photograph by Michelle Binker, courtesy of the *Illinois Valley News*.)

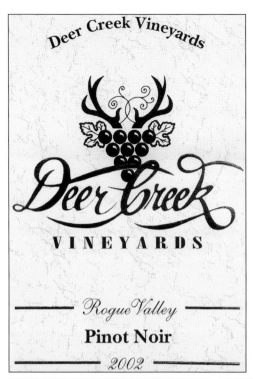

Deer Creek Vineyards was established in 1988 by Ann and Gary Garnett on the 30-acre Daly farm in Selma. The Garnetts put in 8 acres of Chardonnay and 8 acres of Pinot Noir. Their first harvest in 1993 was custom crushed and sold as bulk wine to vintners around the state. Today Deer Creek consists of 40 vineyard acres, including a block of Pinot Gris. Only 800 bottles per year are produced under the estate label seen at left. Below, Ann Garnett is shown among an array of full harvest bins of Pinot Noir. (Both, courtesy of Deer Creek Vineyards.)

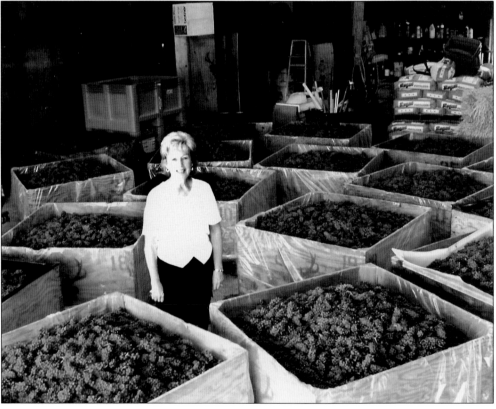

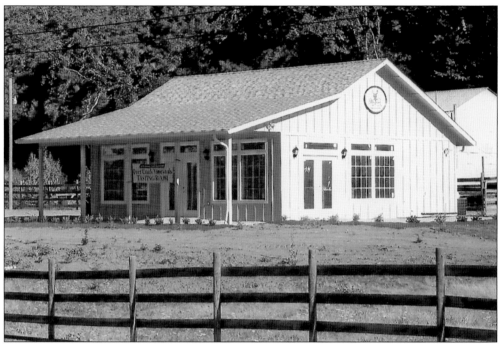

The Deer Creek tasting room (above) stands in the vicinity of Fort Hay, a refuge for white settlers during the Indian wars of 1855 through 1856. Windridge Vineyard of Cave Junction occupies land that used to be part of Fort Briggs, a second place of refuge that existed near Fort Hay during the same period. A historical marker (below) stands along Holland Loop Road to commemorate the erection of the fort in 1854 and the establishment of Josephine County through a bill introduced by state legislator George E. Briggs. (Above, courtesy of Deer Creek Vineyards.)

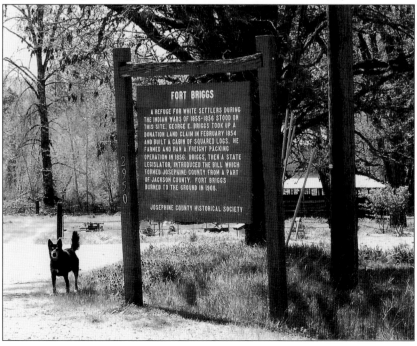

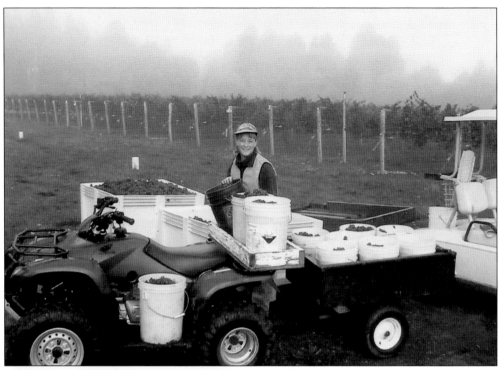

Windridge Vineyard was established in 1989 on property that was once Sucker Creek Ranch, a stud farm. Sucker Creek's Goyamo, who placed fourth in the 1968 Kentucky Derby, is buried on the property. A half-mile racing oval is still visible from the tasting patio. Cate (seen here harvesting fruit) and Terry Bendock acquired the property in 1998, adding to existing plantings of Pinot Noir and putting in Pinot Blanc. (Courtesy of Windridge Vineyard.)

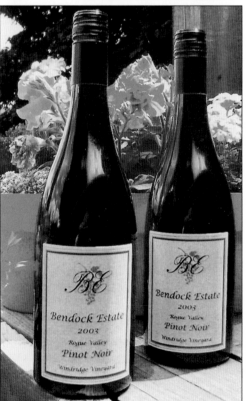

Foris winemaker Sarah Powell admired the Windridge Pinot Noir and produced a first vintage of only 75 cases in 2000. In 2003, the Bendock Estate label was established. After Powell's death in 2004, Terry Bendock took over the winemaking. Bendock Estate wines are 100-percent Pinot Noir, unfiltered and released after two years in bottle. Only 200 cases are made annually. Windridge was sold in 2010, making the estate label a collector's item. (Courtesy of Windridge Vineyard.)

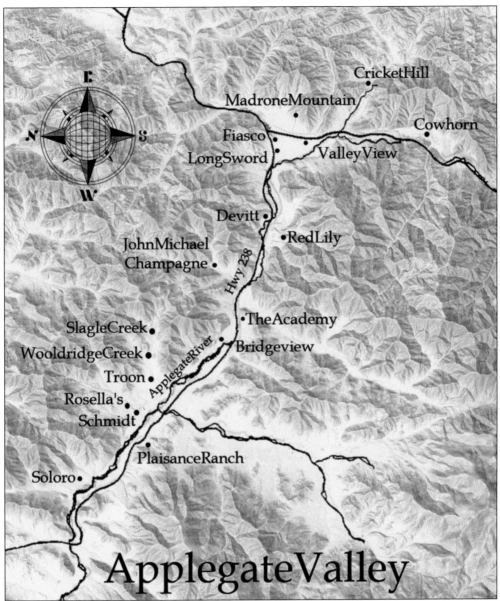

CricketHill

MadroneMountain

Cowhorn

Fiasco

LongSword

ValleyView

Devitt

RedLily

JohnMichael
Champagne

Hwy 238

TheAcademy

SlagleCreek

Bridgeview

WooldridgeCreek

ApplegateRiver

Troon

Rosella's

Schmidt

PlaisanceRanch

Soloro

ApplegateValley

Drier and warmer than the Illinois Valley to the west, the Applegate Valley AVA stretches for 50 miles from the California border to the Rogue River. Following the course of the Applegate River, it encompasses the towns of Ruch and Applegate, extending nearly to Grants Pass. Largely protected from coastal influences and receiving 25 to 45 inches of precipitation annually, the Applegate's vineyards experience a greater number of growing degree days than vineyards in the Illinois Valley. Vineyards are mostly sited on stream terraces with freely draining granitic soils at an average elevation of 1,540 feet. The Applegate is known for Chardonnay and Rhone and Bordeaux varietals. Shown on the map are wineries operating in the region today. Bridgeview of Cave Junction maintains an 80-acre vineyard and tasting room in the Applegate. Not shown is Frank Ferreira's Applegate Red Winery, which was planted in 1997 but closed in 2010. Quady North also is not shown due to the location of its tasting room in Jacksonville, outside of the Applegate AVA. (Map by Adam L. Miller, courtesy of OgdenRoemerWilkerson Architecture.)

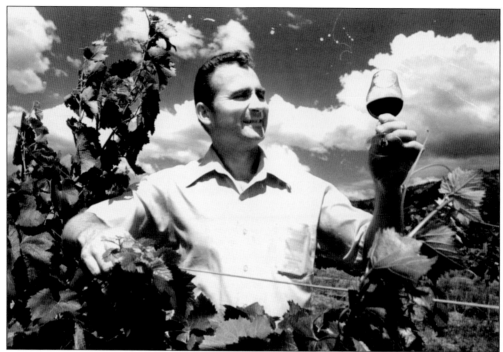

Frank Wisnovsky is pictured in 1979 in his Valley View vineyard. Located near Ruch, the vineyard was given the same name as Peter Britt's early vineyard in Jacksonville. Planted in 1972, Wisnovsky's vineyard represented the first commercial wine grapes in the Rogue Valley since Prohibition. Valley View Winery was licensed in 1978. After he died tragically in 1980, Wisnovsky's operation continued under son Bob and later under sons Mark and Mike. (SOHS #20105, courtesy of the Southern Oregon Historical Society.)

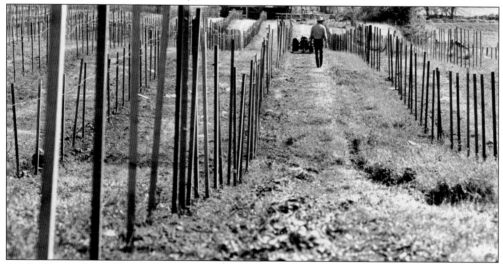

Frank Wisnovsky walks among rows of newly planted cuttings at Valley View. Twelve acres were planted in 1972, with 14 acres added in 1974. The original 26 acres were planted to Cabernet Sauvignon, Merlot, Pinot Noir, and Gewürztraminer. Known for Bordeaux varietals, Valley View has recently expanded its offerings to include Syrah, Viognier, and Tempranillo. (SOHS #20109, courtesy of the Southern Oregon Historical Society.)

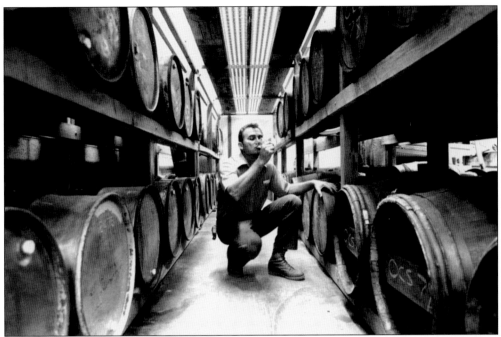

Frank Wisnovsky is shown tasting his 1978 vintage in barrel. In its 35 years, Valley View has had four winemakers. The most recent, John Guerrero, has been with Valley View since 1985. He has served as Valley View's winemaker for over 25 years and also produces his own label, J. F. Guerrero Wines. (SOHS #20104, courtesy of the Southern Oregon Historical Society.)

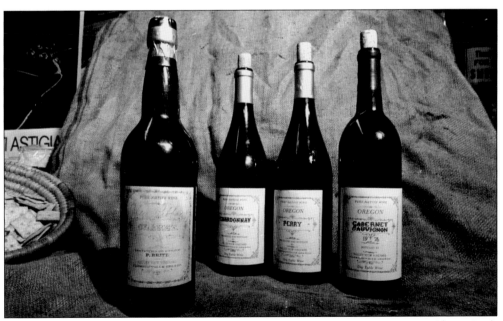

The first modern Valley View vintages are pictured next to a bottle of Peter Britt's Claret. Both modern and antique Valley View labels bear the phrase "Pure Native Wine." The Pioneer label was revived for a limited bottling (160 cases) of the 2005 Merlot to commemorate the 30th anniversary of the modern Valley View. (SOHS #20111, courtesy of the Southern Oregon Historical Society.)

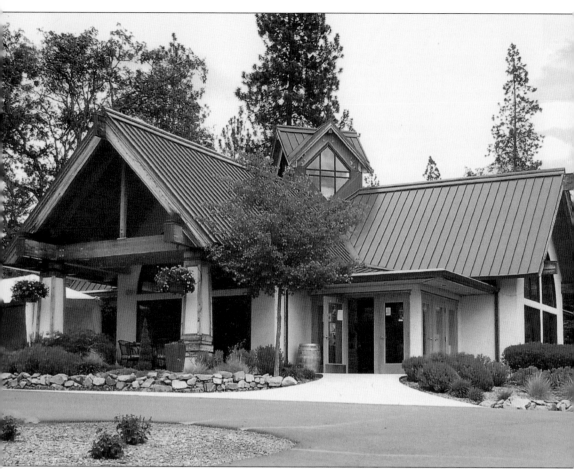

A new wine library and tasting room opened on the Valley View estate in November 2001. The elegant new facility was the culmination of an improvement plan spanning 15 years. New varieties of grapes were planted, and old, less successful ones were pulled out. Higher-quality barrels were purchased, along with a new stemmer/crusher. The Anna Maria label was designated for the highest-quality Valley View vintages. In 2008, Medford *Mail Tribune*'s Cleve Twitchell reported that *Portland Monthly* wine columnist Condé Cox compared the 2005 Anna Maria Tempranillo favorably with a Spanish Tempranillo and found the 2003 Anna Maria Syrah and the 2006 Viognier held their own when tasted side by side with French bottles of the same varietals in an equivalent price range.

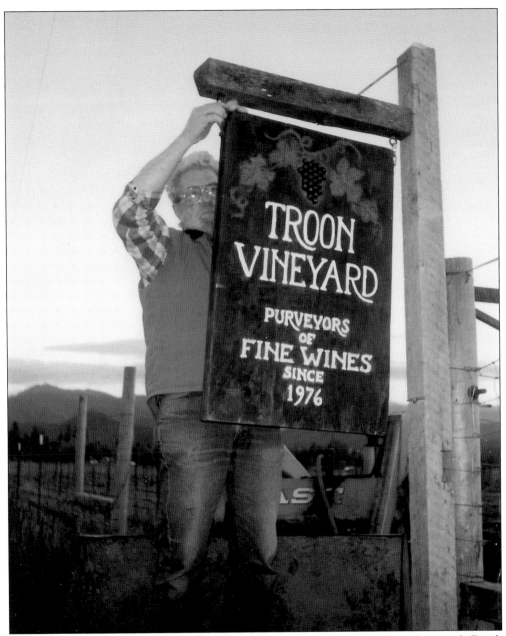

Dick Troon was one of the pioneer viticulturists in the Applegate Valley, along with Frank Wisnovsky and Roger and Barrie Layne. He formulated a course in viticulture for the Grants Pass campus of Rogue Community College. The course—taught by Charles Coury of Forest Grove, Oregon—was attended by students who, for the most part, established their own vineyards and/or wineries. In 1972, Troon planted the original blocks of Cabernet Sauvignon and Zinfandel on his 32-acre property in the Applegate Valley. Troon's first vintages were produced in 1993, a red blend called River Guide Red made by Donna Devine at Siskiyou Vineyard and a Chardonnay made at Bridgeview. Troon also originated Druid's Fluid, a cult wine he calls a "red with training wheels." Known for his sense of humor, Troon is shown here (in 1972) raising his vineyard sign that reads, "Purveyors of fine wines since 1976." (Courtesy of Dick Troon.)

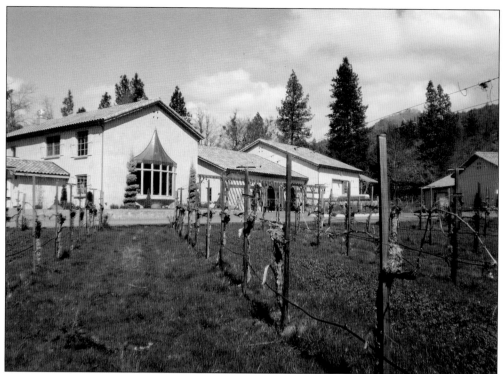

In 2003, the Martin family acquired Troon Vineyard and added 16 acres of Cabernet Franc, Syrah, and Viognier. In 2005, a new 10,000-case winery was completed. Troon's most prestigious varietal remains estate Zinfandel from 20-to-35-year-old vines. The 2002 Zinfandel Estate Grown Reserve Vintage Select won Best New World Zinfandel at the 15th annual Jerry D. Mead's New World International Wine Competition held in Ontario, California, perhaps the highest distinction won by a Southern Oregon wine. (Courtesy of Troon Vineyard.)

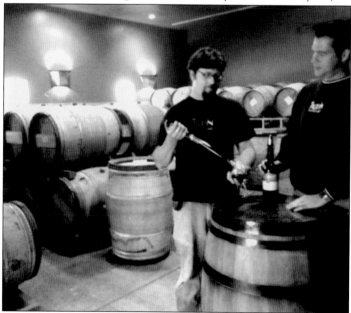

Troon Vineyard's winemaker Herb Quady (left) and owner Chris Martin barrel taste in one of Troon's barrel rooms. Herb Quady is a second-generation winemaker whose father and mother, Andrew and Laurel Quady, began producing Muscat-based dessert wines in the San Joaquin Valley of California in 1975. The Quady family also has an Applegate Valley vineyard and estate label, Quady North. (Courtesy of Troon Vineyard.)

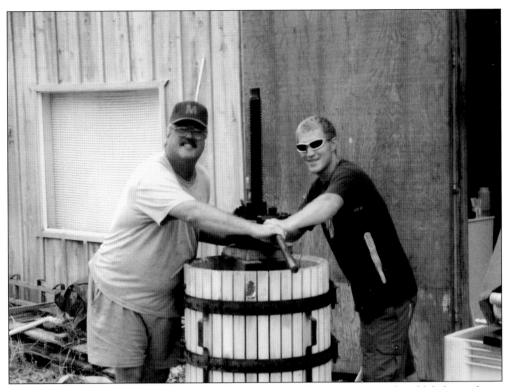

Owner and winemaker Michael Guidici (left) and son John press grapes the old-fashioned way at John Michael Champagne Cellars. Michael Guidici, who has been making wine for 35 years, learned his craft from Geyser Peak's Eddie Gokan. Though he produces a variety of still wines, his specialty is *méthode champenoise.* (Courtesy of John Michael Champagne Cellars.)

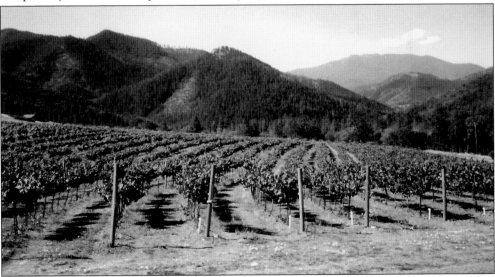

Located in the Applegate Valley on Humbug Creek Road, John Michael's 12-acre vineyard is planted to Pinot Gris, Pinot Blanc, Pinot Noir, Chardonnay, Zinfandel, and Merlot. The tasting room affords a magnificent view of the vineyard, with Grayback Mountain in the background. (Courtesy of John Michael Champagne Cellars.)

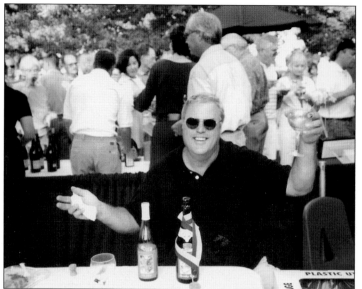

Michael Guidici celebrates at the Oregon State Fair, where his 2003 Champagne won a gold medal. Guidici claims the distinction of having made the only sparkling wine to ever win gold at the event. (Courtesy of John Michael Champagne Cellars.)

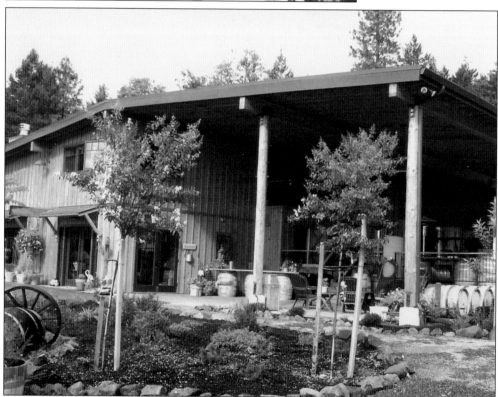

Wooldridge Creek Vineyard and Winery is the collaborative effort of Ted and Mary Warrick, Greg Paneitz, and Kara Olmo. Planted in 1977, the Warricks' original 18-acre vineyard appealed to Paneitz and Olmo, who wanted to establish a winery. The couples joined forces, erecting the winery, which opened in 2005, and expanding the vineyard to 56 acres planted to Cabernet Sauvignon, Merlot, Cabernet Franc, Syrah, Chardonnay, Pinot Noir, Viognier, Sangiovese, Zinfandel, Malbec, Petit Verdot, and Tempranillo. (Courtesy of Wooldridge Creek Vineyard and Winery.)

Winemaker Greg Paneitz, shown in the Wooldridge Creek barrel room, did post-baccalaureate work at Fresno State University and studied at France's National School of Enology in Montpelier. He was interested in establishing his own winery in a spot with climate and geology similar to southern France. The Applegate Valley fit the bill. (Courtesy of Wooldridge Creek Vineyard and Winery.)

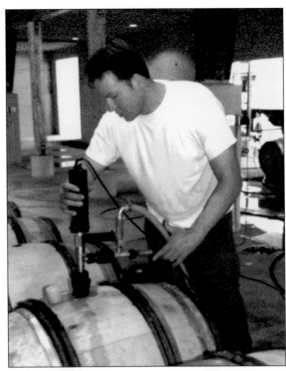

Kara Olmo brings a background in food and marketing to the Wooldridge Creek team. She met Greg Paneitz while doing baccalaureate work in enology at Fresno State University. Here Olmo and Paneitz are blending wine for use in one of Don Mixon's Madrone Mountain dessert wines. (Courtesy of Madrone Mountain.)

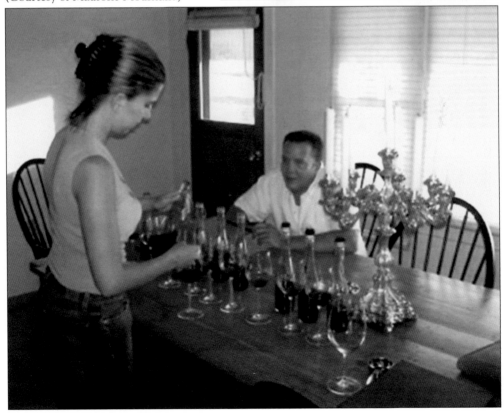

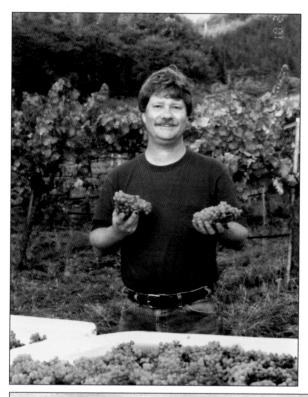

Bob Denman, shown at left with the fruits of his labor, established his Slagle Creek Vineyard in 1980. Farming at low yields, Denman produced top-quality Chardonnay, Merlot, and Syrah for other Oregon vintners until 2001, when he brought out his own label. The Slagle Creek label, below, appears on 2,000 cases per year. The wines were originally made at the Eola Hills Wine Cellars in the Willamette Valley, but today three Rogue Valley vintners— Wooldridge Creek's Greg Peneitz and Kara Olmo and Linda Donovan of the Pallet Wine Company in Medford—are also producing wine from the exceptional fruit of Slagle Creek. (Both, courtesy of Slagle Creek Vineyard.)

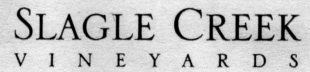

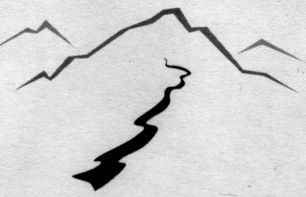

SLAGLE CREEK
V I N E Y A R D S

CHARDONNAY
2004
APPLEGATE VALLEY OREGON

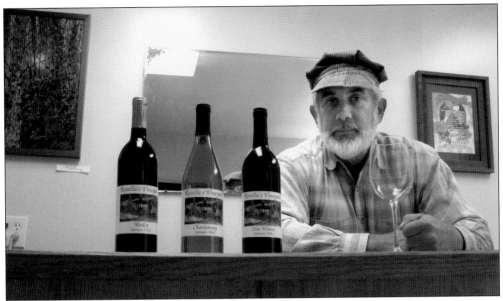

Rosella's Vineyard is a family affair. Planted in 1982, the 8 acres of vines were originally known as Drobney Vineyards. Rex and Sandi Garoutte purchased the vineyard in 1998 and renamed it for Rex's recently deceased mother, Rosella. Rex Garoutte, above, makes Rosella's wines from 100-percent estate fruit. The vineyard produces Cabernet Sauvignon, Merlot, Chardonnay, Zinfandel, and Syrah. Below, nine-year-old Rowdy Garoutte, the owner's son, is shown playing among the vines in 2009. (Both, courtesy of Rosella's Vineyard.)

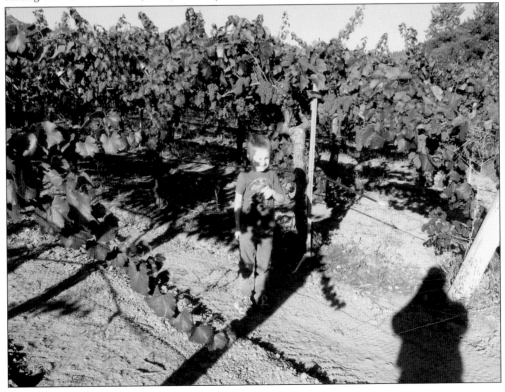

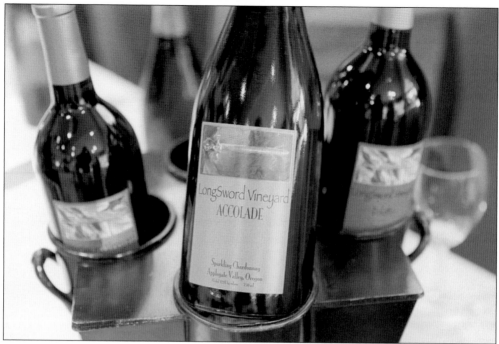

Located just west of Ruch on Highway 238 in the Applegate Valley, LongSword Vineyard takes its name from the English translation of owner Maria Largaespada's Spanish surname. The 10-acre vineyard planted to Chardonnay was established in 1982 by Rick Sharp and acquired by Largaespada and husband Matt Sorensen in 1999. The LongSword label, above, premiered in 2002 on an estate Chardonnay made by Sarah Powell, then winemaker at RoxyAnn Winery. Powell's successor, Gus Janeway, made the 2003 Chardonnay, with subsequent vintages produced at Wooldridge Creek by Greg Paneitz. Below, Maria Largaespada (right) stands with daughter Melinda Fryman next to the vineyard. (Above, courtesy of photographer Steve Addington of Kiaterna Design Group; below, courtesy of LongSword Vineyard.)

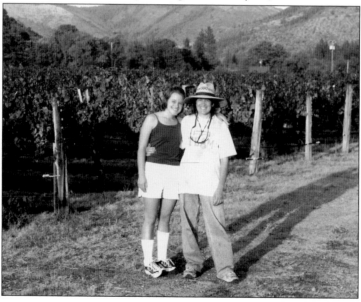

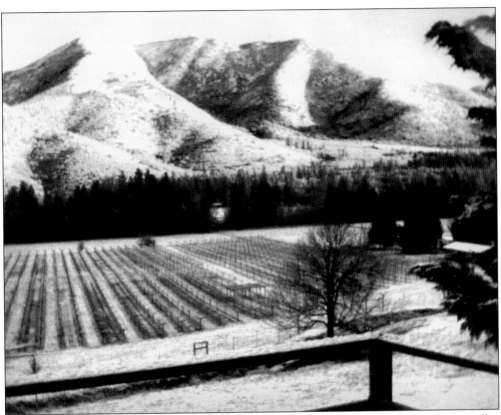

Bernard and Betty Smith, below, established The Academy of Wine in the Applegate Valley after Smith retired from teaching engineering. In 1989, they began planting a 5-acre block with Pinot Noir, Cabernet Sauvignon, Chardonnay, and Merlot. Standing behind Smith's vineyard, above, Billy Mountain shades and cools the vines. "Some say it doesn't suit Pinot Noir here," Smith explained, but he has an American Wine Society gold medal for his 1997 Pinot Noir, which proves otherwise. With a Geneva double-curtain trellis system producing a double canopy, 3,000 vines yield 12 to 13 tons of fruit annually. The rows are spaced wide enough to mow with a full-size tractor, an important point to the Smiths, who do all the vineyard work themselves and produce 300 to 400 cases of estate wine yearly under The Academy of Wine label. (Both, courtesy of The Academy of Wine.)

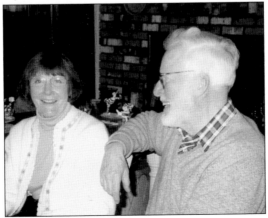

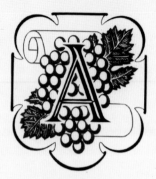

THE ACADEMY

2006
PINOT NOIR

APPLEGATE VALLEY, OREGON
ALCOHOL 13.4 % BY VOLUME

An homage to the French academy system, Smith's label captures his studied approach to viticulture and winemaking. Smith did an apprenticeship at Seven Lakes Vineyard in Fenton, Michigan, before seeking a vineyard site of his own. He later studied enology at the University of California, Davis. (Courtesy of The Academy of Wine.)

After taking enology classes at UC, Davis, and travelling to Bordeaux, France, Duane Bowman (shown amongst cooperage in his Cricket Hill Winery) came to the Applegate Valley. With a vineyard planted to Bordeaux varieties in mind, Bowman found a site on Little Applegate Road with soils and climate similar to the right bank of France's Gironde River.

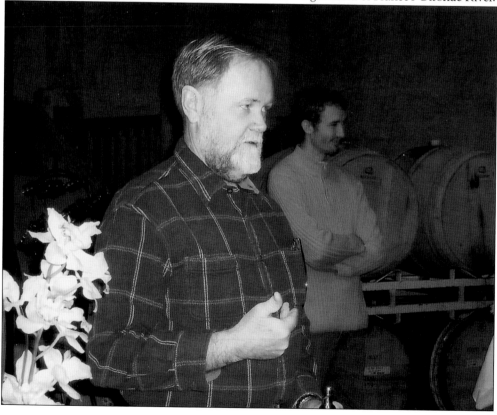

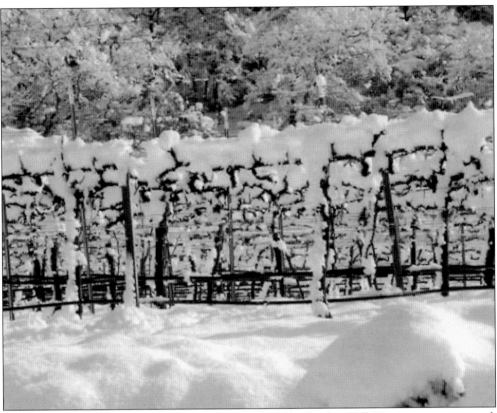

In 1991, Duane Bowman and wife Kathy established the Cricket Hill Winery estate vineyard, planting Merlot and Cabernet Franc cuttings from the St. Emilion and Pomerol regions of Bordeaux. With 2,000 vines to the acre, instead of the usual 1,200, and rows spaced 6 feet apart, the 4-acre vineyard (shown here in snow) flourished. (Courtesy of Cricket Hill Winery.)

In 2001, Bowman began to produce wine under the Cricket Hill label. The Bowmans do all the work in the vineyard and the winery, producing handcrafted vintages that express the varietal heritage, the estate *terroir,* and the winemaker's individuality. The two wines released to date are the 2002 Merlot and Vin Enchanté, a multiyear blend of Merlot and Cabernet Franc. (Courtesy of Cricket Hill Winery.)

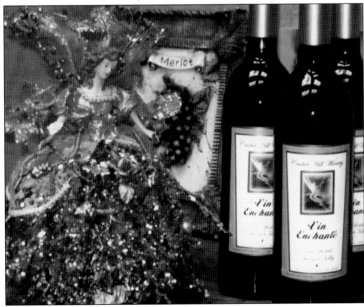

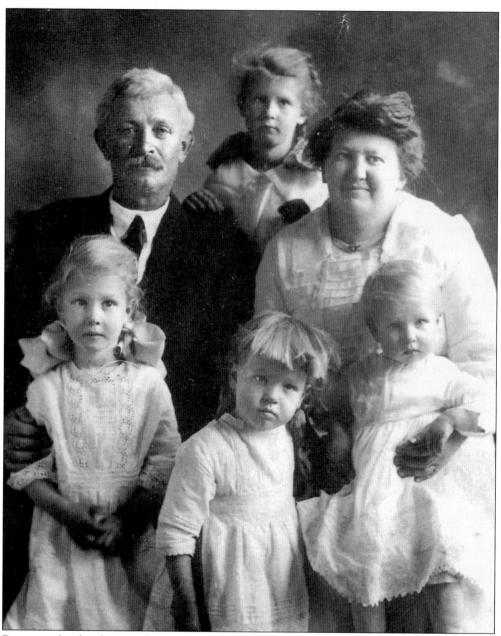

Born to a family of vineyard owners in 1870, Joseph Ginet of Savoie, France, came to Oregon after his discharge from the French army in 1890. In 1898, he established a homestead at Sterling Creek near Jacksonville. Several years later, he returned to France to find a wife but came back to Oregon with cuttings of 28 grape varieties instead. He planted his vineyard and, in 1912, married a mail-order bride of French-Canadian descent, Corinne Valiquette of Idaho. Ginet made wine and sold fruit and grape cuttings from the property he named Plaisance Ranch. He also donated the site for a schoolhouse on a corner of his ranch. The schoolhouse served the district until 1938. Ginet and Corinne are seen here, around 1920, with their four daughters, from left to right, Olivette, Virginia, Josephine, and Francis (standing behind Ginet and Corinne). (Courtesy of Plaisance Ranch.)

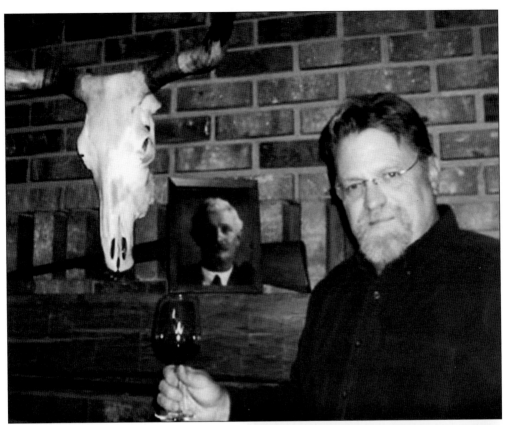

In 1928, Joseph Ginet died before he knew that he had a son. Born two months after his father's death, the second Joseph Ginet died young. The family eventually lost their Sterling Creek property. It fell to grandson Joe Ginet, pictured next to his grandfather's portrait, to reestablish a family vineyard on a new property in Williams. The property was named Plaisance Ranch after his grandfather's place. (Courtesy of Plaisance Ranch.)

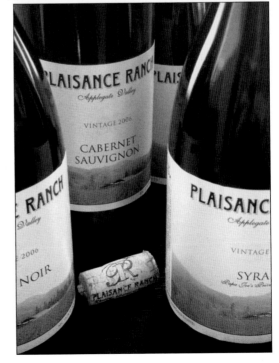

The modern Plaisance Ranch vineyard was planted in 1998 to Cabernet Sauvignon, Pinot Noir, and Syrah. In 2005, Joe Ginet added cuttings of the Mondeuse grape of Savoie imported from France. The winery opened in 2009, with its first vintage a 2006 Rouge Prestige, a blend made primarily of Mondeuse. Also available under the Plaisance Ranch label are the varietals shown here. (Courtesy of Plaisance Ranch.)

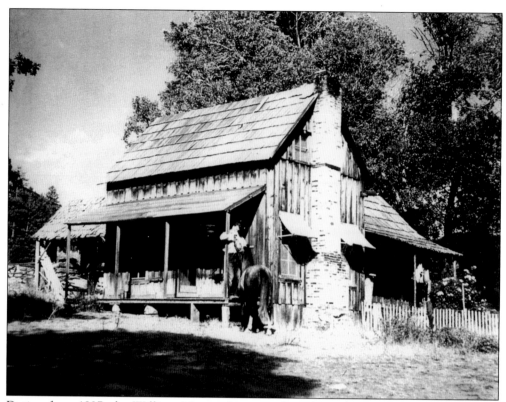

Dating from 1897, the William Matney homestead, with its distinctive board-and-batten construction, serves as the centerpiece of Jacksonville Vineyards. Farmed for over 100 years, this Applegate Valley site became the home and vineyard of Dave and Pamela Palmer, Grants Pass natives who planted vines in 1999. The Palmers restored the Matney homestead as their estate house and have reproduced its style in a newly constructed barrel cellar on the vineyard grounds. (Courtesy of Fiasco Winery.)

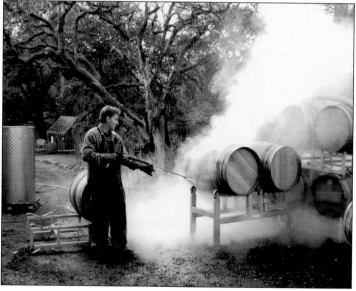

Winemaker and owner Dave Palmer washes down the French oak barrels used exclusively in Jacksonville Vineyards and Fiasco vintages. Using one-third of new cooperage each year, Palmer's Bordeaux wines are aged 24 to 38 months in barrel, while his lighter-style Sangiovese barrel ages for 12 months. (Courtesy of Fiasco Winery.)

The Palmers found this old photograph of an anonymous horn player in the Matney homestead and adopted it as the Jacksonville Vineyards label image. The Fiasco label refers to an old Italian term for round-bottom wine bottles covered in straw. "Committing a fiasco" is a 15th-century expression applied to actors who muffed their lines and were then obliged to pay the fiasco, or buy a bottle of wine, to atone for their forgetfulness. (Courtesy of Fiasco Winery.)

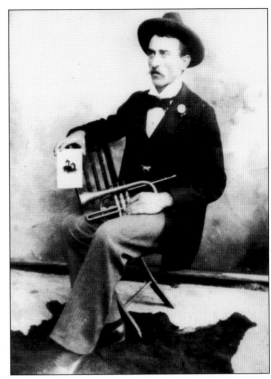

From left to right, Jim and Jeanne Davidian of Caprice Vineyards, Jeff Smith, Lori Dunlap, and Dave and Pamela Palmer taste wine in front of the Fiasco Winery tasting room. Hang gliders in the background reflect Dave's passion for the sport that led him to pursue a career in aviation before becoming a wine grape grower and winemaker. (Courtesy of Fiasco Winery.)

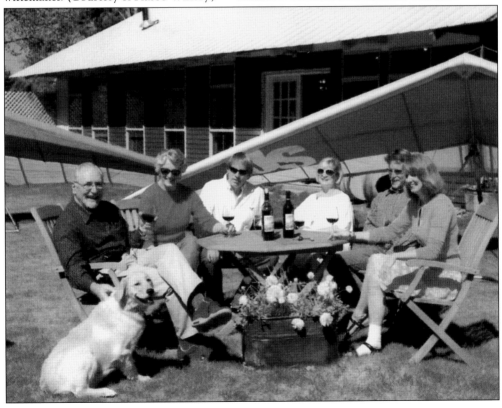

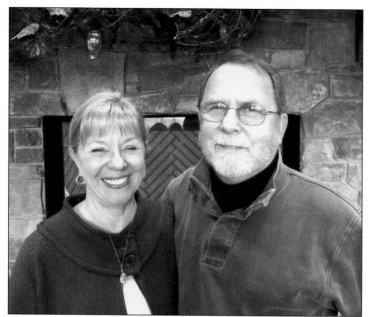

In 2000, Cal and Judy Schmidt purchased the 75-acre Bennett Ranch in the Missouri Flat section of the Applegate Valley. They planted a vineyard to Merlot, Cabernet Sauvignon, and Syrah in 2001. In subsequent years, Malbec, Cabernet Franc, Zinfandel, Chardonnay, Sauvignon Blanc, and Viognier have been added to the original vineyard blocks. Today there are 29 acres in vines. (Courtesy of Schmidt Family Vineyards.)

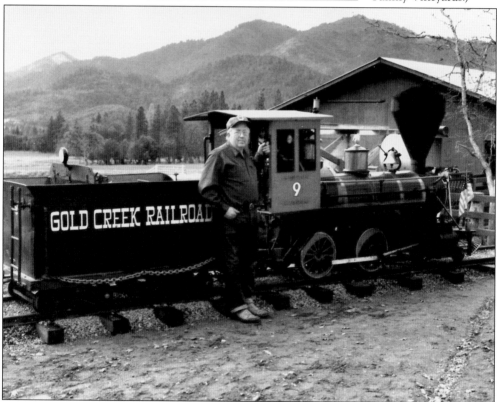

Jack Bennett, previous owner of the Schmidt property, was an avid train buff and collected quarter-scale recreational trains. Bennett laid track around his farm and entertained visitors by taking them for rides on what became known as the Applegate Valley Railroad. (Courtesy of Schmidt Family Vineyards.)

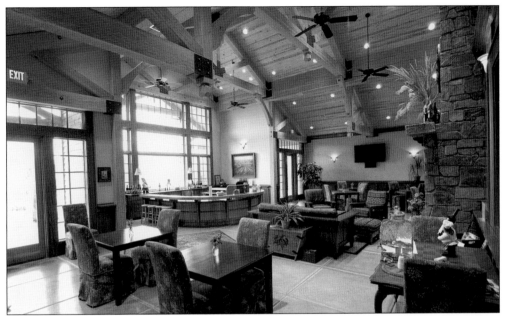

The Schmidt Family Vineyards' winery and tasting room, above, is a lofty Craftsman-style structure surrounded by several acres of herb and flower gardens. Inside, visitors can sample Gewürztraminer, Pinot Gris, Chardonnay, Zinfandel, Merlot, and many award-winning vintages, including the 2008 Viognier and the 2007 Syrah that took silver and gold medals respectively at the 2009 World of Wine Competition. Owner and winemaker Cal Schmidt produces about 1,700 cases annually, 75 percent of which are estate wines. The Schmidt Family Vineyards label, with distinctive botanical illustrations, is shown below on several award-winning bottles. (Above, courtesy of Schmidt Family Vineyards; below, photograph by Teena Jo, courtesy of World of Wine.)

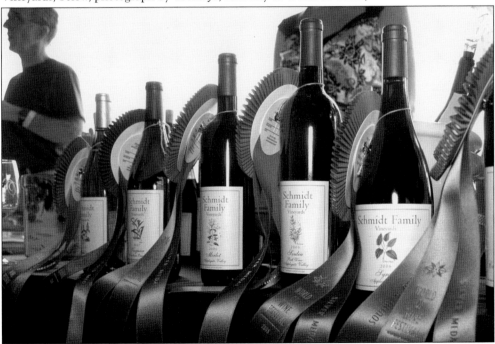

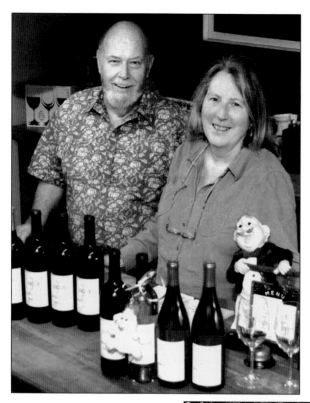

After a stint in Napa County, California, as owner and winemaker of Pope Valley Winery, Jim Devitt and his wife, Sue, came to the Applegate Valley and established a vineyard in 2001. In 2003, they got back into the winery business, and they opened their tasting room in 2004 with one vintage, a Pinot Gris. (Courtesy of Devitt Winery.)

Today the Devitt name, shown on the vineyard sign, appears on 100-percent estate Chardonnay, Merlot, Cabernet Franc, Cabernet Sauvignon, and a dessert wine dubbed "Le Petit Oink." With 10 acres left to plant, the vineyard continues to expand every year. The Devitts welcome visitors to the winery whenever the open sign is out and add that, if visitors call ahead, the sign will definitely be out. (Courtesy of Devitt Winery.)

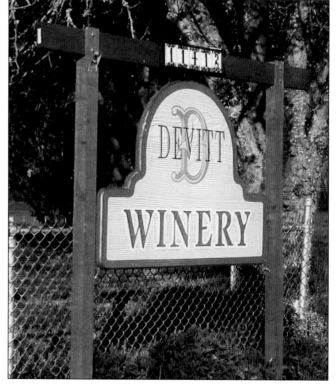

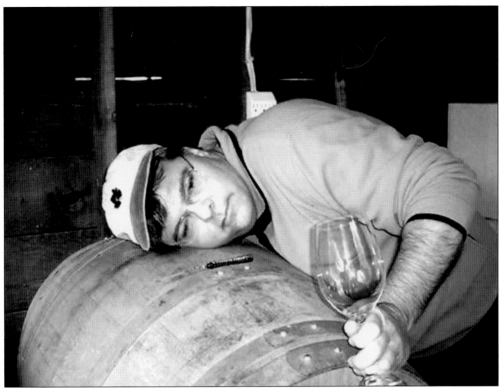

After a 22-year law career, Don Mixon decided to pursue a dream and, with partner Bret Gilmore, bought a vineyard in the Applegate Valley. Madrone Mountain began in 2002 as a small planting of Merlot. Mixon expanded his vineyard and augmented the Merlot with Syrah, Sauvignon Blanc, Riesling, and Touriga Nacional, the most prized Portuguese varietal used in port. Mixon, shown with his ear to a barrel, listens for the fizz of malolactic fermentation. (Courtesy of Madrone Mountain.)

Don Mixon makes the red wine used for his dessert vintages and contracts with Linda Donovan of Pallet Wine Company for the white. The Madrone Mountain label appears on Late Harvest Gewürztraminer; Starthistle Cuvee, a blend of Huxelrebe and old vine Riesling; and Mundo Novo, an Oporto-style blend of Cabernet Sauvignon, Cabernet Franc, and Merlot fortified with brandy. (Courtesy of Madrone Mountain.)

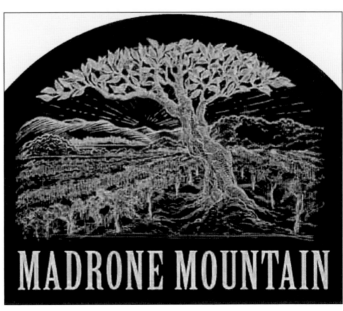

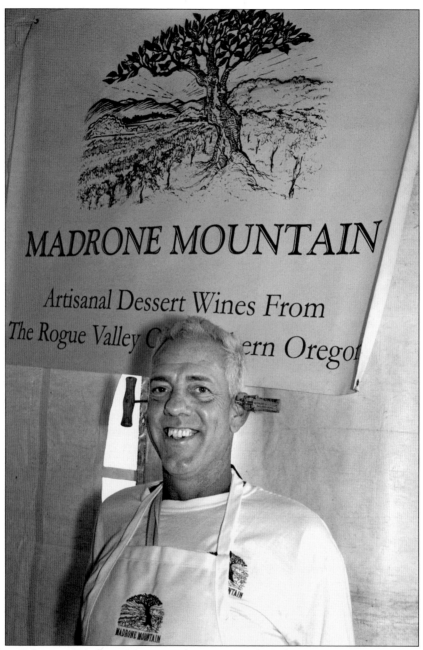

Here Bret Gilmore of Madrone Mountain demonstrates the lighter side of events, like the World of Wine Festival held annually at Del Rio Vineyard in Gold Hill. Co-owner with Don Mixon, Gilmore was pouring Madrone Mountain's artisanal dessert wines at the 2009 festival when this photograph was taken. Established in 2002, Madrone Mountain already enjoys a following and is distributed as far afield as New York City. In 2010, Madrone Mountain produced its first estate wines: a Riesling for use in Starthistle Cuvee and a Touriga Nacional for use in a red dessert wine, Mundo Velho. Madrone Mountain shares a tasting room with Daisy Creek Winery in Central Point, Oregon, next-door to the world famous Rogue Creamery. (Photograph by Teena Jo, courtesy of World of Wine.)

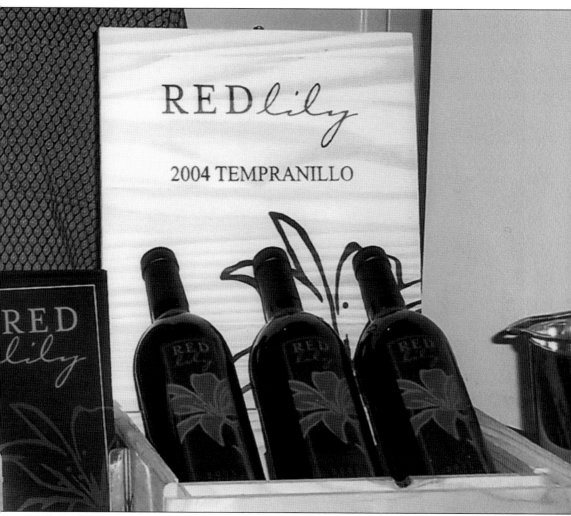

Rachel and Les Martin came to the Applegate Valley with an organic basil farm in mind but decided to grow wine grapes instead. They bought a site and, on advice from viticultural climatologist Gregory V. Jones, planted Tempranillo in 2003. With new vines in the ground, the Red Lily label was established with an inaugural vintage made by Sarah Powell at RoxyAnn Winery from Ellis Vineyards fruit. Rachel Martin learned winemaking as an apprentice to Powell and Gus Janeway and by working the 2008 harvest in Spain. With vineyard expansion to 15 acres, 13 in Tempranillo and 2 in Verdellho, Martin's 2006 Tempranillo and subsequent vintages have been 100-percent estate fruit. Renovation of an old pole barn to serve as the estate tasting room is in the works, and a state-of-the-art winery is in the planning stages. (Courtesy of Red Lily Vineyard.)

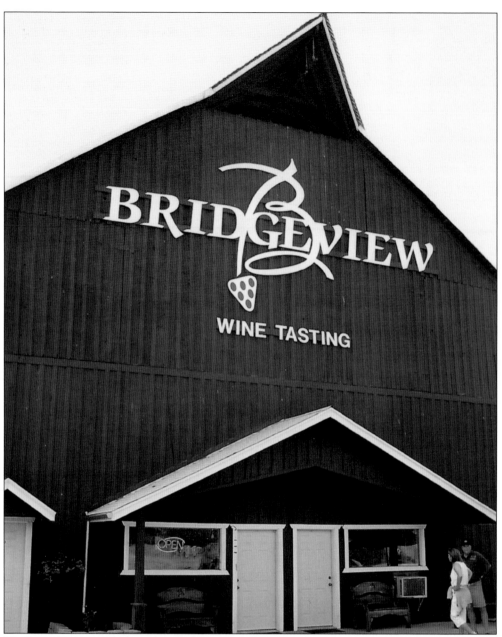

The big red barn visible from the Applegate Valley's Highway 238 is Bridgeview Vineyards' Jackson County tasting room, added in 2004 to Lelo and Bob Kerivan's Cave Junction operation. The adjacent 80 acres of vines consist of Merlot, Cabernet Sauvignon, Chardonnay, Cabernet Franc, Syrah, Riesling, Sangiovese, and a small amount of Viognier used for blending, typically with the Chardonnay. As with the Cave Junction vineyard, pruning ensures that each vine produces fewer grapes with correspondingly greater varietal character. Every aspect of the vineyard operation is carefully managed, from planting to harvest, to encourage flavor intensity. Bridgeview winemaker René Eichmann, who began making wine in Germany, has said that the climate of Southern Oregon makes for a different style of wine, almost a hybrid between Northern California and the Willamette. (Courtesy of Bridgeview Vineyards.)

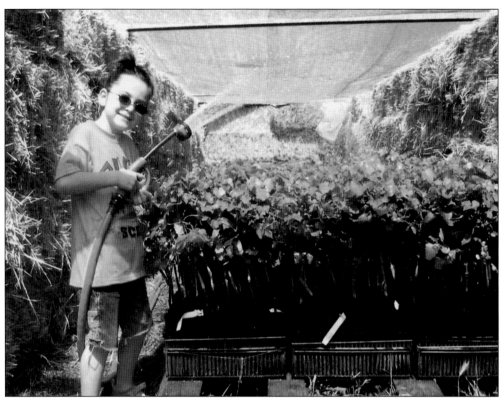

In 2005, the Quady family purchased a 100-acre tract along Highway 238 in the Applegate Valley for the purpose of establishing a vineyard. In 2006, the first 16 acres of the Quady North vineyard were planted to high-quality French clones of Syrah, Cabernet Franc, and Viognier. Herb and Meloney Quady's daughter Margaux helped by watering the young vines prior to their being planted. (Courtesy of Quady North.)

The first Quady North label wines were a pair of Viogniers released in December 2007. The following year, a Syrah and a Cabernet Franc were released. Quady's limited production of these three varietals from purchased fruit earned Quady North a mention in the February 28, 2010, issue of *Wine Spectator*. Both the 2006 Rogue Valley Syrah 4-2, A, and the Applegate Valley Viognier received 90 points. (Courtesy of Quady North.)

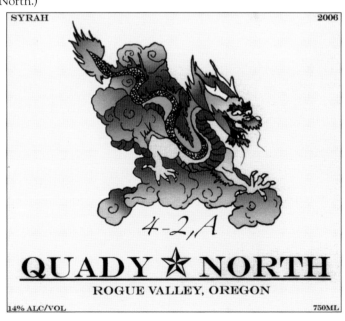

SYRAH   2006

4-2,A

QUADY ★ NORTH

ROGUE VALLEY, OREGON

14% ALC/VOL   750ML

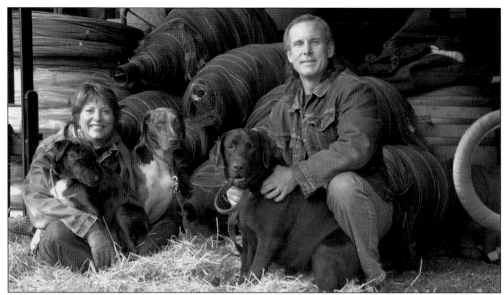

In 2002, Barbara and Bill Steele, above, bought 117 acres of an abandoned dairy farm and established Cowhorn Vineyard and Garden, the only certified organic and Demeter-certified biodynamic wine estate in Southern Oregon. The name is derived from the dairy on the original 1859 Straube Ranch and from the biodynamic process of composting by burying manure-packed cow horns, as demonstrated by Barbara Steele and a vineyard worker (below). Eleven acres chosen for a vineyard by soil assessment and found to be similar to France's Châteauneuf du Pape region were planted in 2005 with Syrah, Viognier, Roussane, Marsanne, and Grenache. Cowhorn's very limited bottling (1,500 to 1,600 cases per year) is made without additives, allowing naturally occurring native yeasts to cause fermentation. (Both, courtesy of Cowhorn Vineyard and Garden.)

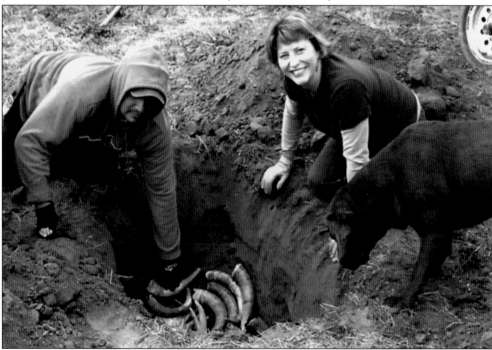

The Cowhorn label, with its spiral logo, was inspired by the shape of a cow's horn. Cowhorn vintages made by Bill Steel have garnered accolades from *Wine Spectator*, which gave the 2007 Viognier a 90-point rating and notoriety as far away as New York City, where the James Beard House recently poured the 2006 Syrah and the 2008 Spiral 36, a blend of Marsanne, Roussanne, and Viognier. (Courtesy of Cowhorn Vineyard and Garden.)

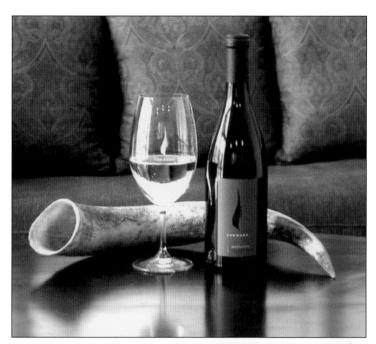

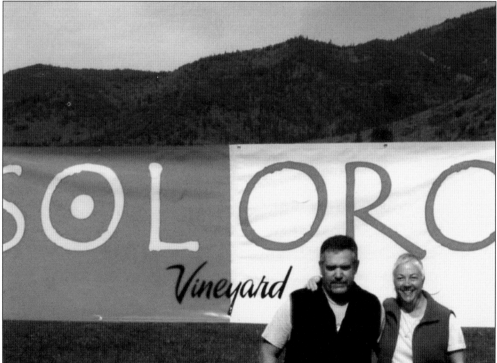

Like so many other vineyard and winery owners, Jim and June Navarro (an operating room nurse and judicial assistant respectively) had long dreamed of growing grapes and making wine. In 2006, half of the dream came true when they planted their Soloro Vineyard, located in the Applegate Valley on North Applegate Road, to Syrah, Grenache Noir, Rousanne, Marsanne, and Viognier. (Courtesy of Soloro Vineyard.)

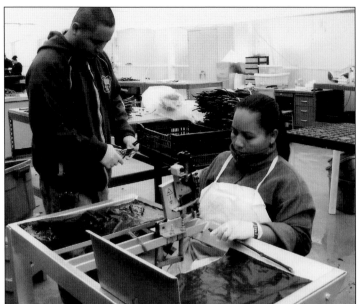

Soloro's Rhone varietals were imported by Tablas Creek from Chateau de Beaucastle through Novavine of Santa Rosa, California. Novavine technicians are pictured machine-grafting the varietal cuttings onto rootstock specifically chosen to suit the soils on the site where they will be planted. Soloro's first estate vintage was a 2008 blend of Marsanne and Viognier named Thunderegg Cut. (Courtesy of Soloro Vineyard.)

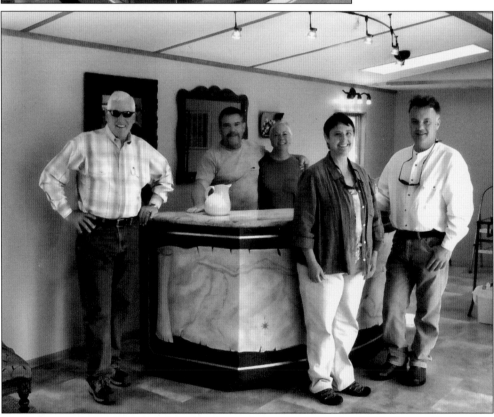

The Soloro tasting room, located on the vineyard property, opened in 2008. Pictured behind the counter are the Navarros. In the foreground are friend Andy Pearl (left) and the tasting room's first customers. Wines are made by Steve Anderson of Eola Hills in the Willamette Valley and Linda Donovan of Pallet Wine Company in Medford. (Courtesy of Soloro Vineyard.)

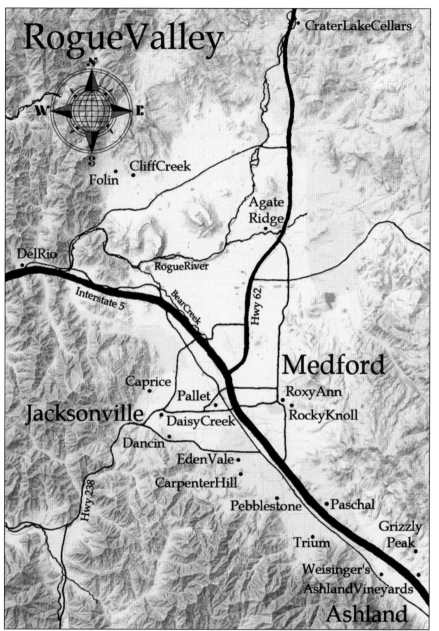

The valley of the Rogue River and its tributary Bear Creek form the easternmost section of the Rogue Valley AVA. Flanking the Interstate 5 corridor, this area surrounds Ashland, Jacksonville, Medford, Gold Hill, Rogue River, Eagle Point, and Shady Cove. A total of 15 to 25 inches of precipitation falls annually, making this the driest part of the Rogue Valley AVA. The vineyards around Bear Creek are at the highest elevations, averaging 1,752 feet. Average elevation farther north in the main valley of the Rogue is 1,102 feet. Cooler, higher elevation sites are well suited to Bordeaux and Burgundy varieties. Rhone varieties thrive in warmer, lower elevation sites. Shown on the map are wineries operating in the region today. South Stage Cellars, the label associated with Don and Traute Moore's Quail Run Vineyards, has a tasting room in Jacksonville. (Map by Adam L. Miller, courtesy of OgdenRoemerWilkerson Architecture.)

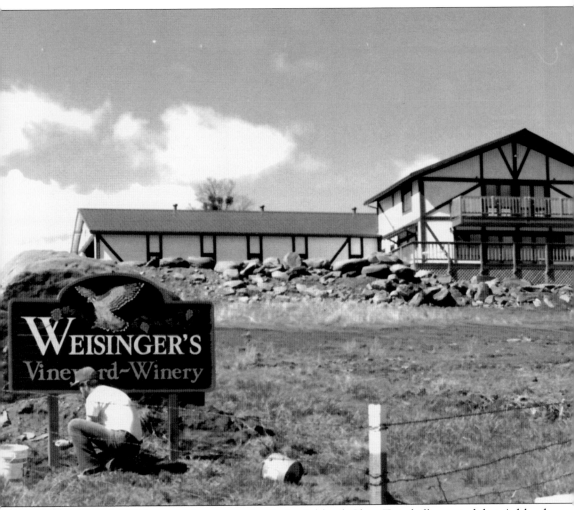

In a 1988 *Mail Tribune* article on new wineries in Ashland, Cleve Twitchell reported that Ashland Vineyards' Bill and Melba Knowles were building a winery next to their 4 acres of Pinot Noir and Riesling and that Sherita and John Wiesinger had also sited a winery and tasting room on their nine-year-old vineyard. John Weisinger is shown putting up the sign for his new winery on the south side of Ashland. Originally from Texas, Weisinger came to Ashland after stints in Alaska and Klamath Falls, Oregon. He took up the vineyard and winery business after a career as a Presbyterian minister and youth counselor. Started in 1979 from Gewürztraminer cuttings obtained from Frank Wisnovsky, Weisinger's vineyard now consists of 4 acres planted to Pinot Noir, Gewürztraminer, and Tempranillo. At 2,100 feet, Weisinger's is one of the highest vineyard locations in the Rogue Valley. (Courtesy of Weisinger's of Ashland.)

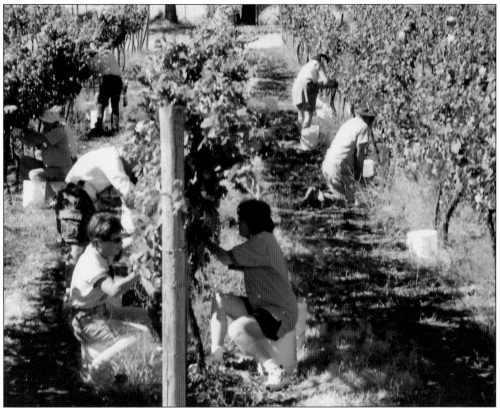

As with many small wineries, Weisinger's accepts volunteer help at harvest time to minimize labor costs and offer friends and patrons an opportunity to experience this exciting time in the vineyard. Above, volunteers are shown harvesting estate-grown Gewürztraminer. The display below was made to show the volunteer workforce how to pick grapes and demonstrates that an example is worth a thousand words. (Both, courtesy of Weisinger's of Ashland.)

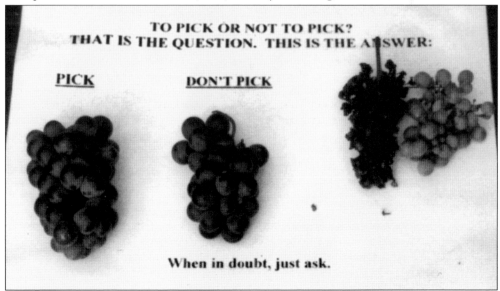

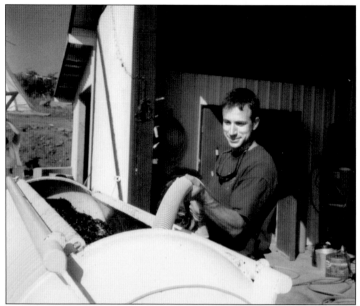

Eric Weisinger, the founder's son and winemaker at Weisinger's from 1998 to 2006, is shown in 1997, while still an assistant winemaker, pressing off Gewürztraminer. Eric is a member of a second generation of Southern Oregon wine industry professionals, along with Mark and Mike Wisnovsky of Valley View and Gregory V. Jones, whose father Earl founded Abecela Winery in the Umpqua Valley. (Courtesy of Weisinger's of Ashland.)

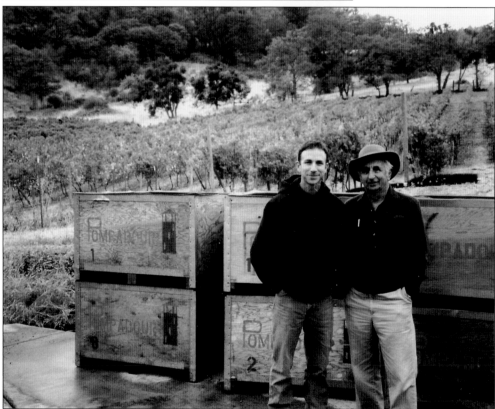

Winemaker Eric Weisinger and the late Rogue Valley wine grape grower Arnold Kohnert stand on the crush pad at Weisinger's as the fruit from Kohnert's Pompador Vineyard is delivered. Kohnert's fruit, now produced under the management of Randy Gold, is used for Weisinger's highly regarded Petite Pompador Bordeaux blend.

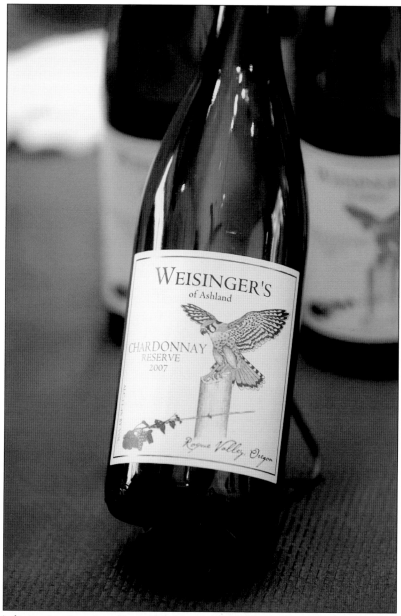

Weisinger's distinctive American Kestrel label is used for its white wines, which include Chardonnay, Semillon-Chardonnay, Pinot Gris, Gewürztraminer, and Viognier. The kestrel appears embossed in silver on the purple red wine label. Weisinger's red wines include Cabernet Sauvignon, Cabernet Franc, Petite Pompadour (a Bordeaux blend), Syrah, Pinot Noir, and a port-style wine named Barille. Donna Devine, formerly of Siskiyou Vineyards, made Weisinger's first vintage, the 1988 Gewürztraminer. Eric Weisinger became winemaker in 1998. His 2005 Reserve Cabernet Sauvignon was singled out by *Wine Press Northwest* on September 11, 2009, as one of the "Fab Cabs" of Washington, Oregon, British Columbia, and Idaho. The article noted that Eric Weisinger has excelled in making Bordeaux varieties over the years. In 2006, he left the family winery to embark on a career as a winemaking consultant. He now splits his time between working with wineries in Southern Oregon and New Zealand. (Courtesy of Steve Addington of Kiaterna Design Group.)

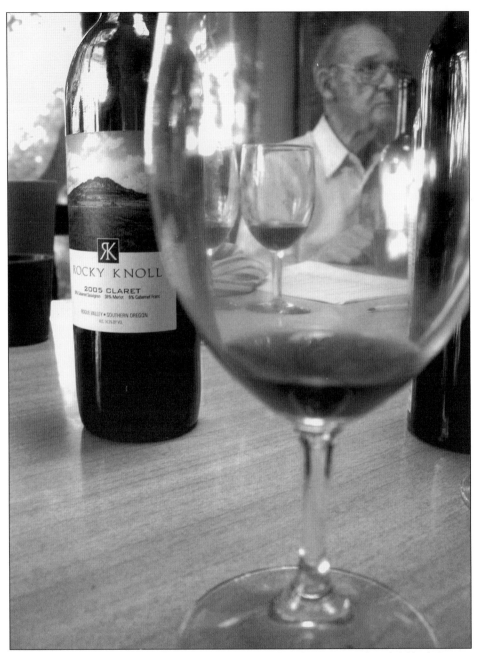

At the urging of Hillcrest Orchard's Reginald Parsons, brothers Leonard and Alfred Carpenter bought property in the Rogue Valley and put in a pear orchard, using draft horse teams, in 1909. In 1946, Dunbar Carpenter returned to Medford after a stint in the army during World War II and took over the business. In the mid-1970s, pears gave way to wine grapes. By 2006, there were four generations, including Dunbar's daughters Emily and Karen and granddaughter Ali, working Rocky Knoll. Rocky Knoll Vineyard's founder, the late Dunbar Carpenter, was photographed through a wine glass next to a bottle of Rocky Knoll's inaugural vintage, the 2005 Claret. The 2005 estate Claret is a blend of Cabernet Sauvignon, Cabernet Franc, and Merlot made by Gus Janeway while he was winemaker at RoxyAnn Winery. (Courtesy of Rocky Knoll.)

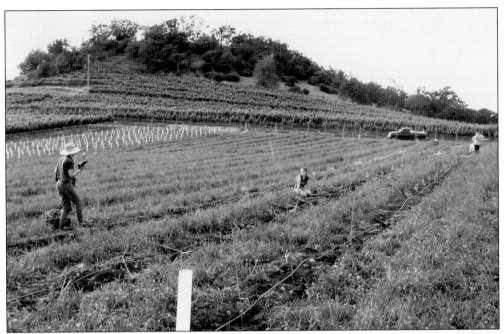

Made from vines as old as 35 years, Rocky Knoll Claret demonstrates the balance and complexity of old vine fruit from the south-facing slope on the label. The slope is terraced east-to-west below exposed outcrops of sandstone. Located in one of the hottest and driest parts of the Rogue Valley, Rocky Knoll produces well-ripened, intensely flavored Bordeaux varietals. (Courtesy of Rocky Knoll.)

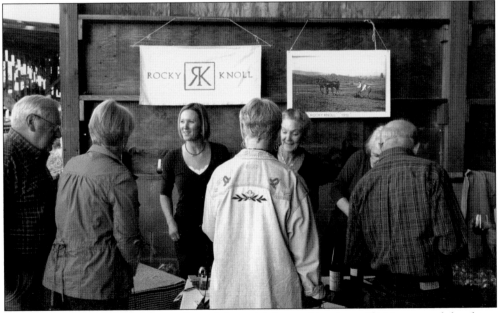

Dunbar Carpenter's descendants, (from left to right) granddaughter Ali Mostue and daughters Emily Mostue and Karen Allen, pour Rocky Knoll wines for vineyard visitors. Behind them on the barn door is a banner made from an old photograph of forebears Leonard and Alfred Carpenter using a draft horse team to break ground for their pear orchard. (Courtesy of Rocky Knoll.)

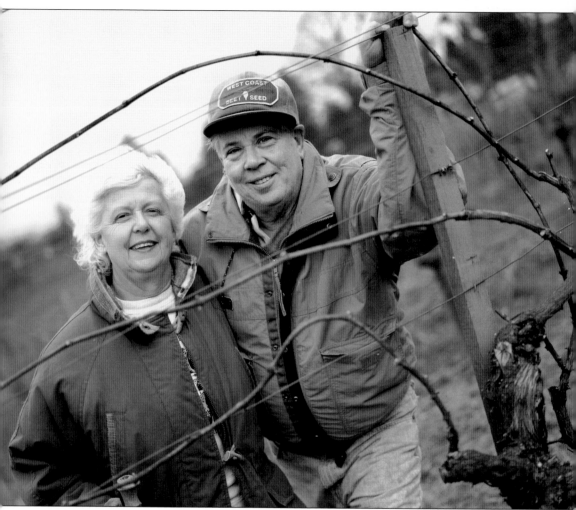

In 1989, Don and Traute Moore moved to Talent, purchased the original 13 acres of Quail Run Vineyards, and began experimenting with varietals. Their holdings expanded over the years to 12 vineyards totaling 280 acres in several diverse microclimates of the Rogue Valley. Quail Run produces over 20 varietals, most of which go to make award-winning wines produced by Willamette Valley wineries. Perhaps the most well known of the labels sourced from Quail Run is Griffin Creek, a line of Bordeaux- and Rhone-style wines produced since 1998 by Joe Dobbes at Willamette Valley Vineyards. The *Wine Enthusiast* gave the inaugural Griffin Creek Merlot a score of 90 out of 100. In 2006, the Moores established their estate label, South Stage Cellars. Wine judge and columnist Lorn Razanno of Ashland called the initial South Stage offerings superstars more than worth the price. (Courtesy of South Stage Cellars.)

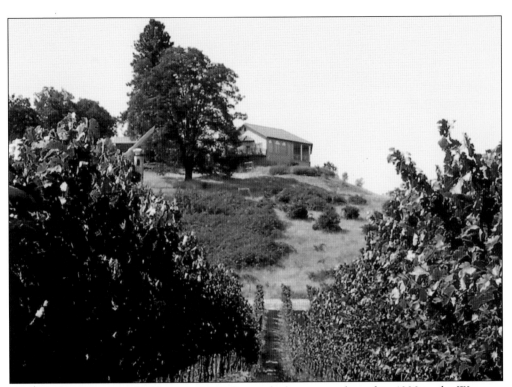

Kurt and Laura Lotspeich's Pheasant Hill Vineyard, above, was planted in 1990 in the Wagoner Creek drainage above Talent. For years they sold their entire harvest to various wineries until, in 2003, they combined forces with Nancy Tappan's Evans Creek Vineyard and Randy Gold's Gold Vineyard to produce an estate label, Trium (Latin for "of the three"). Trium's inaugural vintage, the 2003 Growers' Cuvee, was awarded the platinum medal and best of show at the 2005 Greatest of the Grape competition. Randy Gold has since left the partnership to pursue his vineyard management business full time. Today Trium's 1,000 cases of Pinot Gris, Viognier, Merlot, Cabernet Sauvignon, Cabernet Franc, and Growers' Cuvee are produced from Pheasant Hill and Evans Creek fruit exclusively. The tasting room located at Pheasant Hill, below, is open to the public. (Both, courtesy of Trium.)

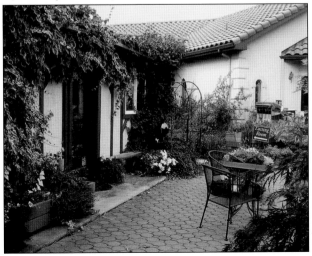

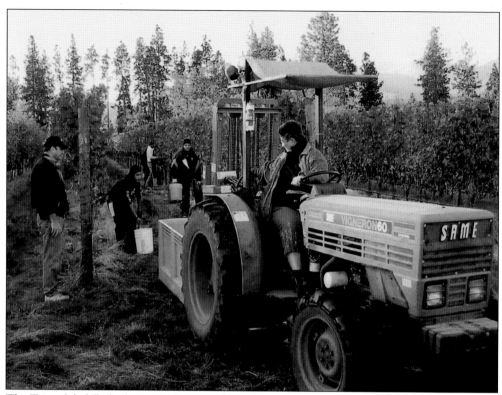

The Trium label (below), a reproduction of a 16th-century woodcut depicting a vineyard worker, expresses the hard labor involved in growing premium wine grapes. Laura Lotspeich (above), shown driving a tractor and directing the work of a vineyard crew, writes that when she and Kurt set out to start a vineyard, "We tested soils, researched trellises, plowed, tilled, cut out blackberries, chased out cows and enlisted everyone in the family and all willing friends to help." The Trium partners agree that the hard work pays off in the glass. Trium wines are produced by winemaker Kiley Evans through a custom crush agreement with Agate Ridge Vineyards. (Above, courtesy of Velocity Cellars; below, courtesy of Trium.)

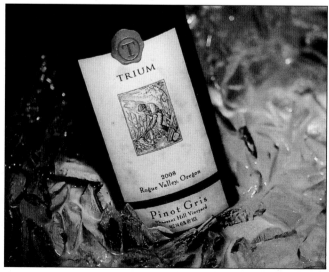

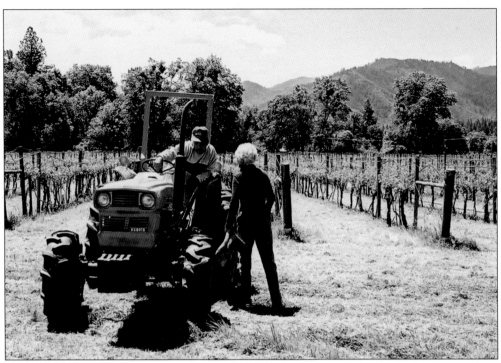

Above, Nancy Tappan, owner of Evans Creek Vineyard, confers with vineyard manager Juan Rios. Located near the city of Rogue River, Evans Creek Vineyard was planted in 1984 to Cabernet Sauvignon, Merlot, and Cabernet Franc. The first fruit was sold to Weisinger's of Ashland. Evans Creek Vineyard is not to be confused with Evans Valley Vineyard, situated 20 miles east of the city of Rogue River and owned by the Ellis Mott family. Evans Valley introduced its first wine in 1986, a Pinot Noir Blanc by Valley View winemaker John Guerrero, but disappeared from the scene within several years. Below, the finest fruit from Evans Creek Vineyard goes into Trium wines, poured by Nancy Tappan (left) at the 2010 Oregon Cheese Festival with Trium tasting room assistant Cheryl Lashley. (Above, courtesy of Evans Creek Vineyard.)

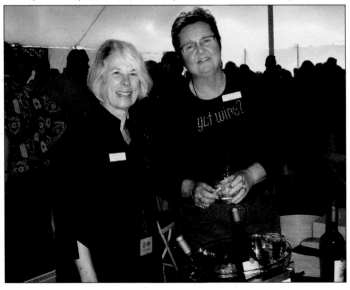

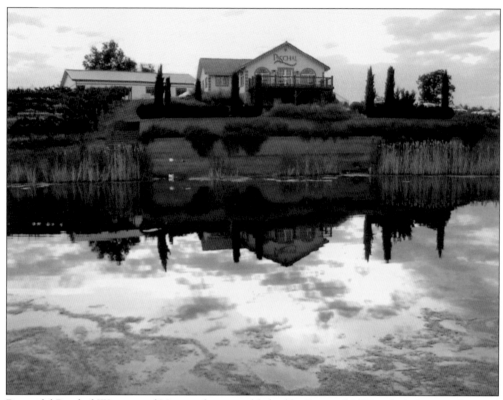

Beautiful Paschal Winery and Vineyard was established by Roy and Jill Paschal. Owner of several radio stations in Alaska, Roy Paschal jokingly calls himself an absentee owner who didn't know how to spell wine. The 13-acre estate just south of Medford was planted around 1990 to Pinot Noir and Chardonnay. (Courtesy of Ed Dunsavage.)

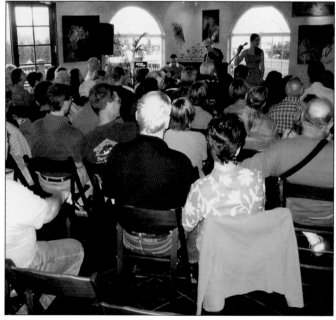

Gus Janeway was the original Paschal winemaker. When he left in 2001, Paschal vintages were made by Joe Dobbes of Dundee, Oregon. Ron Tenuta, a third-generation winemaker with an enology degree from UC, Davis, and experience in a 15,000-case winery in California, and wife Donna acquired Paschal in 2009. Wine may soon be produced on the estate, which for many years has hosted musical events, such as this performance by the Jessica Fichot Group of Los Angeles presented by the Siskiyou Institute. (Courtesy of Ed Dunsavage.)

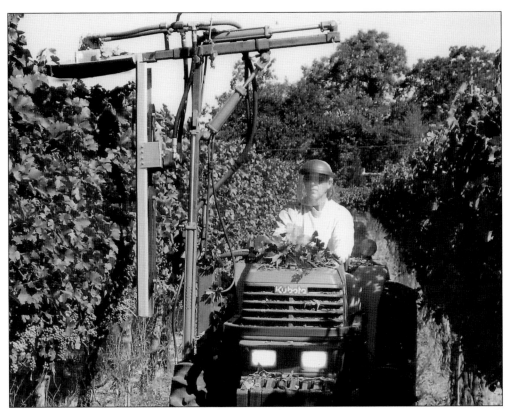

Located north of Phoenix on an ancient stream bed at an elevation of 1,650 feet, Ellis Vineyards was planted to Pinot Gris, Syrah, Tempranillo, Merlot, Cabernet Sauvignon, and Cabernet Franc when Dick and Pat Ellis acquired it in 2003. Having experienced viticulture on a friend's vineyard in Calistoga, California, and bottled wine as home winemakers since 1981, the Ellises knew how much work a commercial vineyard would entail. Above, Dick Ellis is shown trimming the canopy of the vines, a process known as hedging. Later in the season, Pat Ellis, below, is decked out to begin the harvest. The Ellises added a block of Viognier in 2004, bringing the total vineyard acreage to 15.5. They decided to begin making wine commercially under their own label, Pebblestone Cellars, that same year. (Both, courtesy of Pebblestone Cellars.)

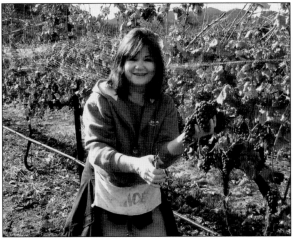

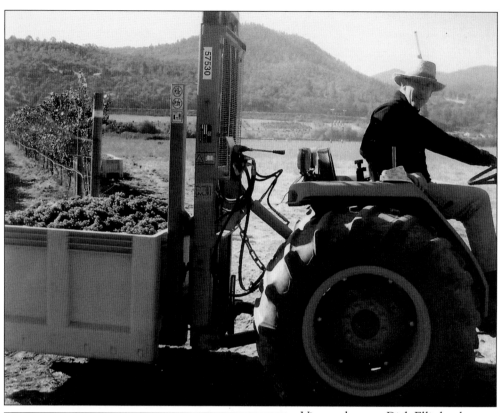

Vineyard owner Dick Ellis hauls a harvest bin, about half a ton, of grapes for transport to the winery via flatbed truck. Each year, about 75 percent of the Ellis Vineyards harvest is sold to other wineries. The balance is used to produce Pebblestone Cellars vintages. Pebblestone wines are 100-percent estate fruit made by winemaker Bryan Wilson of Foris by custom crush agreement. (Courtesy of Pebblestone Cellars.)

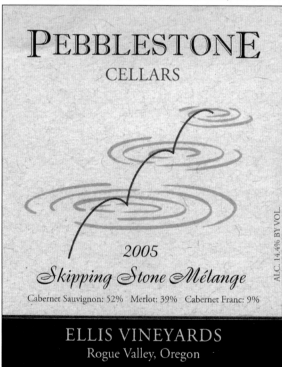

PEBBLESTONE

CELLARS

ALC. 14.4% BY VOL.

2005
Skipping Stone Mélange

Cabernet Sauvignon: 52%   Merlot: 39%   Cabernet Franc: 9%

ELLIS VINEYARDS
Rogue Valley, Oregon

Pebblestone produces about 1,000 cases a year. To date, a Viognier, Pinot Gris, Merlot, Cabernet Franc, Syrah, and Mélange (a Bordeaux blend) have been released. Pebblestone's barrel protocol for reds calls for 18 to 20 months in French oak, 25 percent of which is new cooperage. (Courtesy of Pebblestone Cellars.)

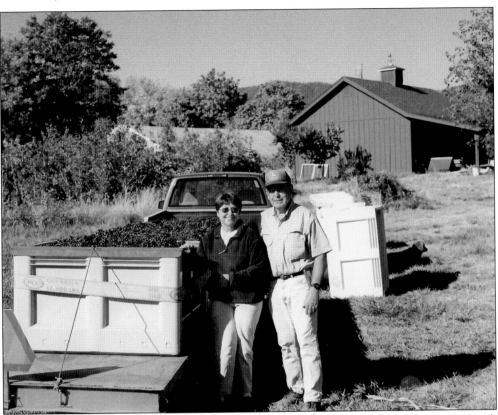

Russ and Margaret Lyon, above, came to Jacksonville in 1997 and established Daisy Creek Vineyard on property where remains of a slurry mine attest to fortune seekers panning for gold in the 1850s. They chose their site for its similarity to the Côte Rôtie of the Rhone Valley and have built their reputation on premium Syrah and award-winning Viognier. The wines produced under the Daisy Creek label, below, are made by Kiley Evans through a custom crush agreement with Agate Ridge. (Both, courtesy of Daisy Creek Vineyard.)

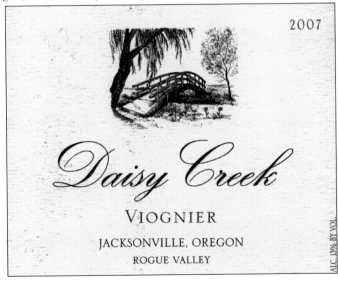

2007

Daisy Creek

VIOGNIER

JACKSONVILLE, OREGON

ROGUE VALLEY

ALC. 13% BY VOL.

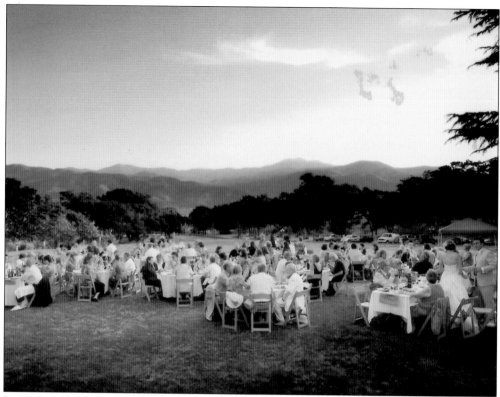

In 1998, in the deep clay of the bottomland flanking Grizzly Peak northeast of Ashland, Al and Virginia Silbowitz established a 15-acre vineyard at an elevation of 2,200 feet. The Silbowitzs designed their grounds with special events in mind. Ashlander Myles Rogers and Barb Kaufman chose the Grizzly Peak winery grounds for the site of their wedding in 2008. (Photograph by Bryon Devore, courtesy of Grizzly Peak Winery.)

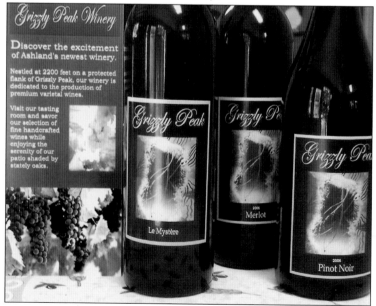

Wines bottled under Grizzly Peak's Celebration label by artist Nancy Holley are available in the estate tasting room. Opened in 2008, the tasting room offers a selection of estate wines produced in quantities of less than 100 cases per varietal. In the works is a new estate winery that will be powered by a photovoltaic farm. Production will still be limited to 3,000 cases per year.

Following a stint in the Willamette Valley, winemaker Andy Swan joined Ashland Vineyards in 1991, then moved to Henry Estate Winery before coming to Grizzly Peak in 2006. Swan's Grizzly Peak wines include a crisp Chardonnay, Pinot Gris, Pinot Noir, Bordeaux reds in a rich, comfortable style, Rhone varietals, and a Tempranillo. He also makes his personal label, Granite Peak, on-site, hence the advertising phrase "two great wineries under one roof." (Courtesy of Granite Peak Winery.)

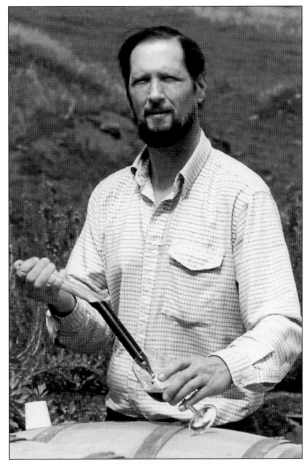

The Rock Point Stage Hotel was built in 1864 by L. J. White on land acquired from J. B. White, who had received the parcel as payment for his service in the 1855 and 1856 Rogue Indian Wars. The hotel opened to the public in 1865. It was renovated to serve as a tasting room by Del Rio Vineyards owners Rob and Jolee Wallace and Lee Traynam. (SOHS #4882, courtesy of Southern Oregon Historical Society.)

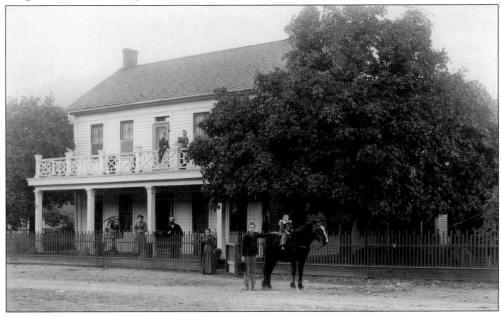

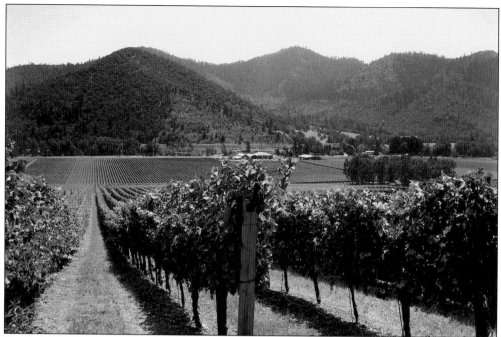

Planted in 1998 on 185 acres on the north side of the Rogue River at Gold Hill, Del Rio Vineyards grows 14 varieties of grapes, primarily warm-climate, with Syrah predominating. At 1,000 feet of elevation, the south-facing slopes benefit from daytime warmth and cool nights, ensuring well-ripened fruit with good acidity. (Courtesy of Del Rio Vineyards and Winery.)

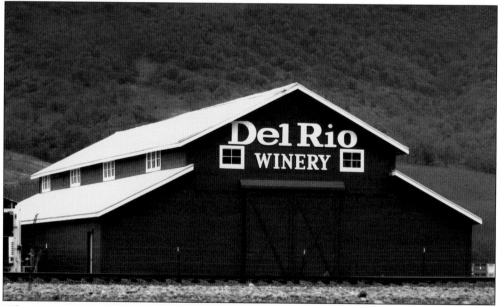

What was once the Del Rio Orchard packinghouse is today the Del Rio Winery. Although most of the Del Rio harvest is sold to some 40 wineries in Oregon, California, and Washington, some fruit is held back for the estate label. French winemaker Jean-Michel Jussiaume produces Del Rio Winery's premium Viognier, Pinot Noir, and Chardonnay. (Courtesy of Del Rio Vineyards and Winery.)

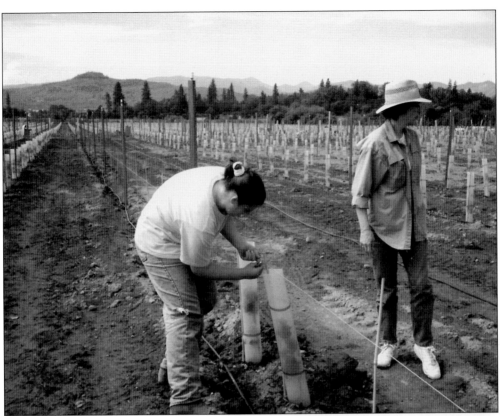

Just north of Gold Hill, Sam's Valley Vineyard was established in 1999 by the late Vern Garvin, pioneer of Oregon's cable television industry. Granddaughter Kelly Garvin (left) installs grow tubes around newly planted grape vines with Kathleen Warren, wife of the minister who blessed the vineyard. The original 15 acres have grown to 70, planted to Merlot, Cabernet Sauvignon, Cabernet Franc, Syrah, and Sangiovese. (Courtesy of Cliff Creek Cellars.)

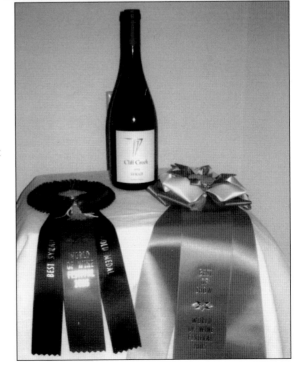

The Garvins' estate label, Cliff Creek Cellars, is made by Joe Dobbes of Dundee, Oregon. In its first year of commercial production, Cliff Creek 2003 Syrah took Best of Show and Gold at the 2005 World of Wine Festival, held at Del Rio Vineyard in Gold Hill, Oregon. The 2004 Syrah scored 90 points and the 2004 Claret 89 points in *Wine Spectator*. (Courtesy of Cliff Creek Cellars.)

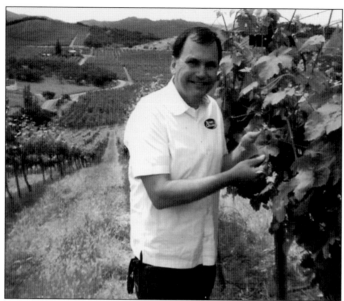

In 1998, Lee and Vicki Mankin planted Carpenter Hill Vineyard on a steep, east-facing slope at the base of the Siskiyou Mountains. The 25-acre site in Medford produces Merlot, Syrah, Petite Sirah, and Roussanne. Since 2004, Carpenter Hill estate wines have been made by Laurent Montalieu of McMinnville, Oregon. David Gremmells inspects Carpenter Hill Syrah leaves for use in wrapping Rogue Creamery cheese. (Courtesy of Carpenter Hill Vineyard.)

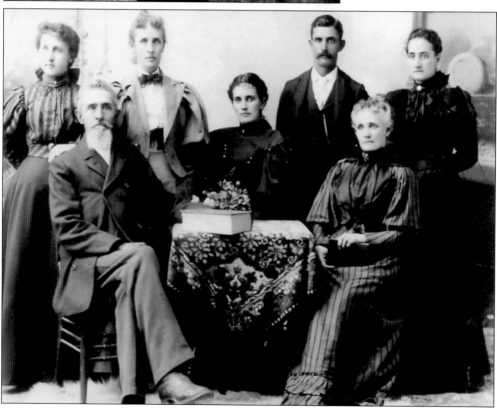

The Stewart family founded Eden Valley Orchards on the property where Eden Vale Winery is now located. Joseph H. Stewart, father of the commercial pear industry in Southern Oregon, planted the 160-acre parcel in pears, almonds, plums, and apples. In 1887, the Oregon and California Railroad was completed, making it possible to sell commercial carloads of fruit as far away as New York City. (Courtesy of Eden Vale Winery.)

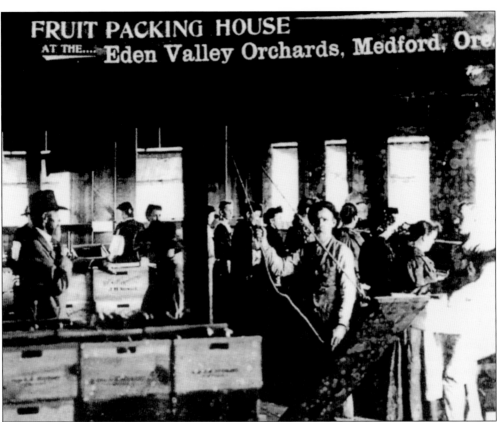

FRUIT PACKING HOUSE
AT THE... Eden Valley Orchards, Medford, Ore

Many hands were needed in the packinghouse at the Eden Valley Orchard. In 1912, the Medford Commercial Club reported that the orchard broke all records for quantity, shipping 40 cars of pears from 48 acres, which averaged $2 a box, or $40,000 for the crop. (Courtesy of Eden Vale Winery.)

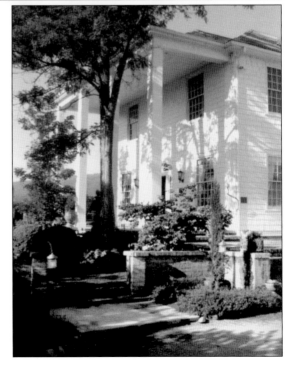

In 1899, Joseph H. Stewart sold Eden Valley to Gordon Voorhies. Voorhies expanded the orchard to 800 acres and, in 1925, remodeled the estate mansion in Colonial Revival style. In 1999, Anne and Tim Root acquired the property, later opening the Voorhies mansion and grounds to the public. The Roots had the entire property placed on the National Register of Historic Places on July 14, 2000. (Courtesy of Eden Vale Winery.)

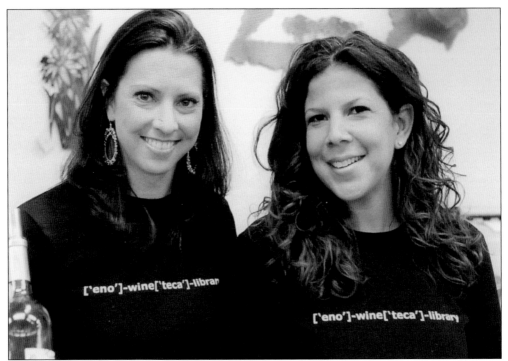

Ashley Campenella (left), winemaker at Eden Vale since 2008, produces wines under the Eden Vale and Pear House Collection labels. Wines are available for tasting on the estate and at Enoteca in Ashland, which is managed by Misty Santos (right). (Courtesy of Eden Vale Winery.)

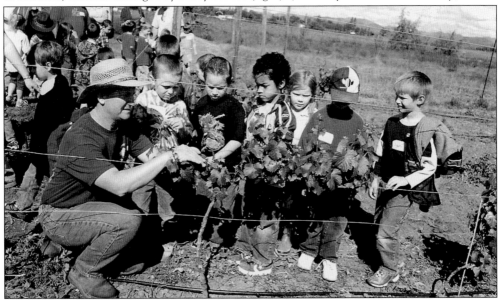

Mary and Steve Gardner purchased a hay farm on Highway 62 near Eagle Point and broke ground for vines with a 1949 Ford 8N tractor that Mary's grandfather had used on his farm. They planted Merlot, Cabernet Sauvignon, Pinot Blanc, Chardonnay, Mourvèdre, and Teroldego, a varietal from Trentino, Italy. Chemist and winemaker Steve Gardner explains the growth of grape vines to son Austin's kindergarten class. (Courtesy of Crater Lake Cellars.)

Further demonstrating a penchant for recycling, the Gardners established Crater Lake Cellars winery and tasting room in what was once a firehouse. The 1956 District No. 4 leather fire helmet is featured on the label of Crater Lake Cellars Fire House No. 4, a red blend. Proceeds from each bottle benefit the fire district in its new home. (Courtesy of Crater Lake Cellars.)

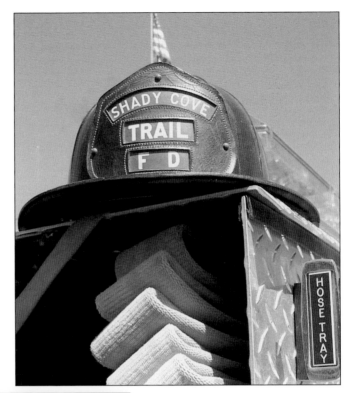

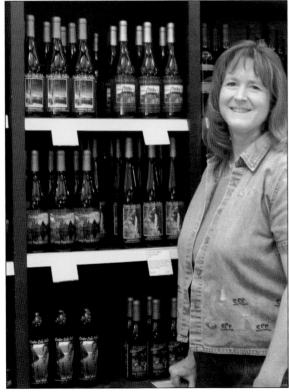

Winery owner Mary Gardner stands next to a selection of Crater Lake Cellars vintages in the winery tasting room in downtown Shady Cove. Each wine has a different picture on the label, many featuring a stunning Crater Lake vista or an antique of one sort or another, each with a story Mary is eager to share with visitors. (Courtesy of Crater Lake Cellars.)

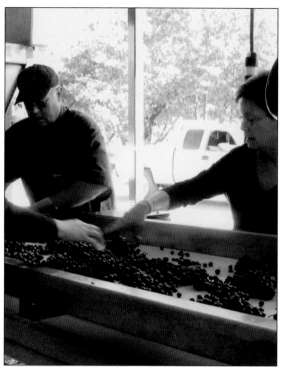

Folin Cellars owners Scott and Loraine Folin sort grapes from the 2009 harvest. They converted their baby kiwi/alfalfa farm to a 25-acre vineyard in 2001. Located about 10 miles north of Medford at an elevation of 1,300 to 1,450 feet, the vineyard is planted to Viognier, Syrah, Tempranillo, Petite Sirah, Mourvèdre, and Grenache. (Courtesy of Folin Cellars.)

Folin Cellars winery was designed to facilitate high-end winemaking, with caves placed 10 feet underground to minimize energy needed for heating and cooling and a harvest deck at ground level to allow processing by gravity feed. The tasting room, opened in 2009, occupies the main floor. Built with open beam ceilings and large windows, the room captures natural light and affords beautiful views of Sam's Valley. (Courtesy of Folin Cellars.)

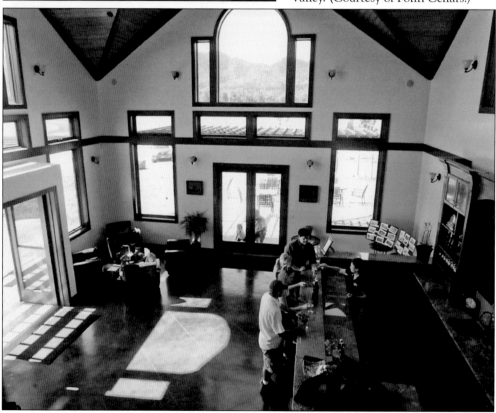

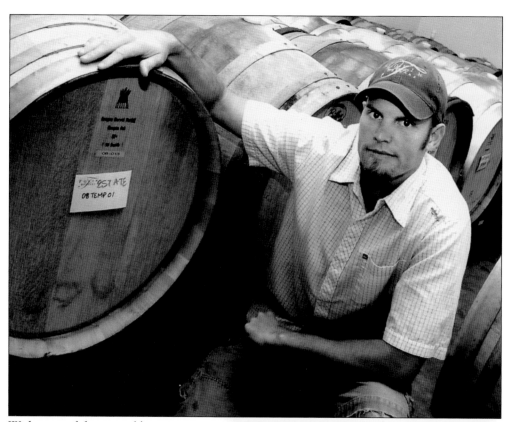

With most of the annual harvest contracted to other wineries, Folin Cellars produces 500 cases yearly using minimal intervention in the winemaking. Bottles are sealed with a glass device, the Vino Seal, hence the phrase "No Cork, No Worries" on the back label. Winemaker Rob Folin, shown above in the barrel room, believes in using gentle winemaking techniques that emphasize the unique character of varietals produced on the Sam's Valley estate. After working in the Willamette Valley for seven vintages, Folin helped his parents map out a plan to establish a vineyard and winery on their farm. Folin produced his first commercial vintage under the Folin label, right, in 2005. (Both, courtesy of Folin Cellars.)

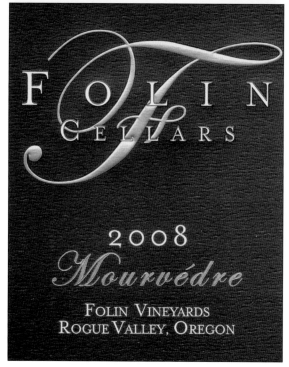

FOLIN CELLARS

2008
Mourvèdre

FOLIN VINEYARDS
ROGUE VALLEY, OREGON

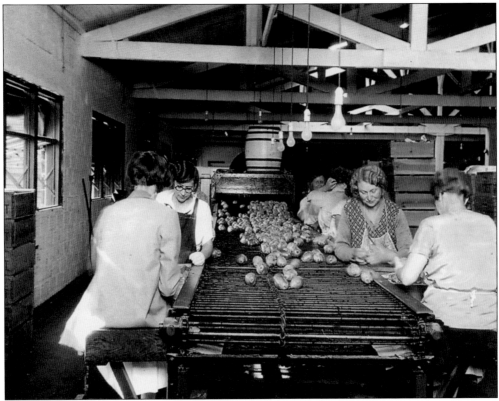

In 1908, Reginald H. Parsons purchased Hillcrest Orchard from J. W. Perkins. Parsons added new varieties of pears, apples, and peaches and quickly established a reputation as one of the finest orchards in the Rogue Valley. Workers are shown packing Hillcrest fruit. Many of the original Hillcrest Orchard buildings were placed on the National Register of Historic Places in 1984 and are in use today as assets of RoxyAnn Winery. (Courtesy of RoxyAnn Winery.)

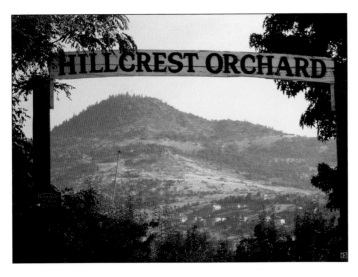

Established in 2002, RoxyAnn Winery is named for RoxyAnn Peak outside Medford. Part of Hillcrest Orchard, the vineyard property is located in shallow limestone-clay soils on the southern exposure of RoxyAnn Peak. Conditions are ideally suited to Cabernet Sauvignon, Malbec, Merlot, Cabernet Franc, Grenache, Tempranillo, Viognier, and Syrah. (Courtesy of RoxyAnn Winery.)

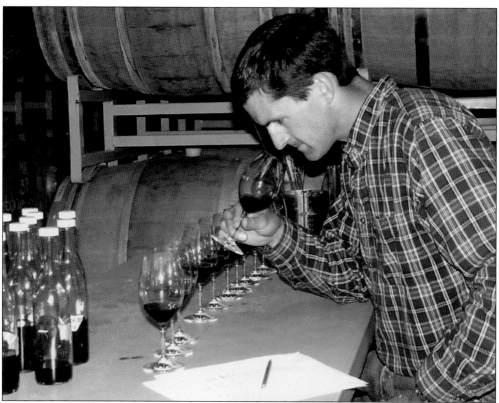

Shown above blending wine, Gus Janeway succeeded Sarah Powell as RoxyAnn winemaker in 2003 after serving as vineyard manager at Don Moore's Quail Run Vineyards and founding winemaker at Paschal Winery. Janeway produced critically acclaimed wines for RoxyAnn and for several custom crush clients, including Carpenter Hill, Red Lily, Rocky Knoll, Daisy Creek, and Volcano Vineyards. He left RoxyAnn in 2009 to focus exclusively on his own label, Velocity Cellars. Shown at right in the vineyard is current RoxyAnn winemaker John Quinones. Quinones follows in the tradition of Sarah Powell and Gus Janeway. "A winemaker," he says, "can't create wines that surpass the quality of the fruit. With appropriate viticultural practices, desired flavor profiles, balance and texture can be developed in the vineyard, long before the grapes are brought into the winery." (Above, courtesy of Velocity Cellars; right, courtesy of RoxyAnn Winery.)

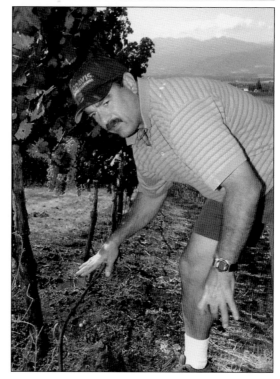

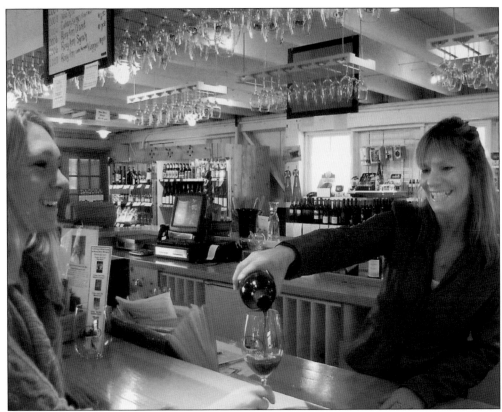

Brenda Crissie pours for visitors in the RoxyAnn tasting room, housed in the old Hillcrest Orchard barn. RoxyAnn estate wines made from the extraordinary Bordeaux and Rhone varietals grown at Hillcrest exhibit tremendous color, complexity, and depth of flavor. RoxyAnn's first winemaker, Sarah Powell, stressed ripeness, richness, and concentration, a style characteristic of today's vintages. (Courtesy of RoxyAnn Winery.)

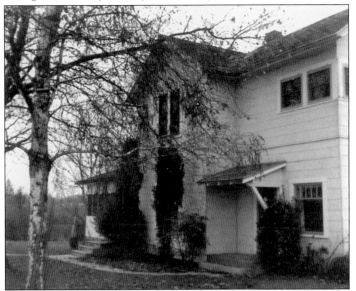

Located on 126 acres farmed by the Dugan family for over a century, Agate Ridge Vineyard is a prime example of preservation of farm-use-designated land through viticulture. Located near the Table Rocks outside Eagle Point, the 30-acre vineyard was planted by the Kinderman family in 2002. The Dugan homestead, pictured in 1964, is preserved as a tasting room for vintages made at the estate winery since 2005. (Courtesy of Agate Ridge Vineyard.)

At right, farmer's daughter Margaret Dugan is shown driving a tractor back in the days when the farm produced wheat. Below, in today's Agate Ridge winery, winemaker Kiley Evans (left) discusses bottling procedures with volunteer workers Debbie Woolf (left) and Glorianne Nicholson. There were 225 cases of 2008 estate Primitivo bottled for release in 2010. Primitivo is a lower-alcohol Zinfandel made by Evans to achieve exceptional acid balance with supple tannins and delicate aromatics. (Right, courtesy of Agate Ridge Vineyard.)

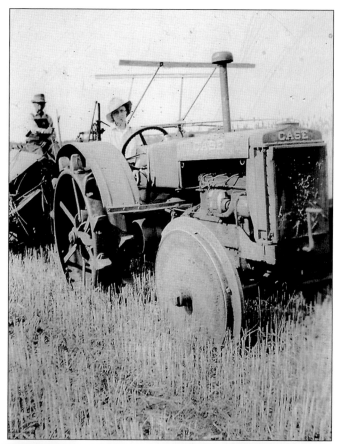

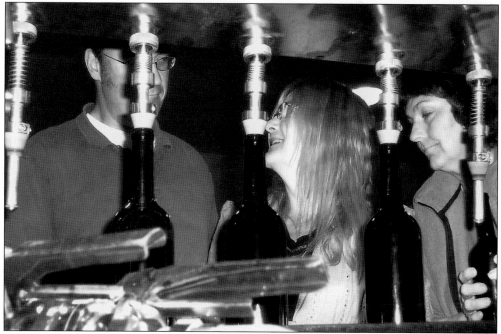

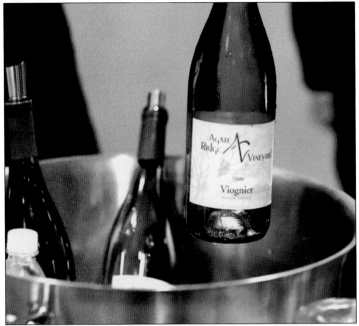

The first winemaker at Agate Ridge was Linda Donovan in 2004 and 2005, followed by Dr. Willard Brown in 2006 and 2007. Under current winemaker Kiley Evans, the Agate Ridge label has gained recognition for Rhone varietals such as Viognier, Roussanne, Marsanne, Syrah, and Grenache. Other estate wines include Sauvignon Blanc, Petite Sirah, Zinfandel, Malbec, and Cabernet Sauvignon. (Photograph by Steve Addington, courtesy of Kiaterna Design Group.)

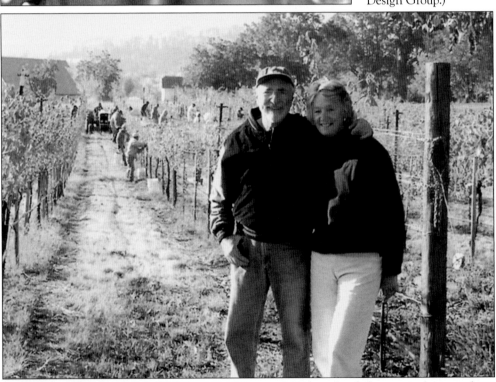

Riverside, California, alpaca ranchers Jim and Jeanne Davidian decided to move their ranching operation to Oregon in 2004. They bought a property with a vineyard outside Jacksonville. The vines, planted around 1990 by Tony Migliarese, were mostly Cabernet Sauvignon and some Chardonnay. The Davidians, shown in their vineyard at harvest, decided to make wine in 2005. (Courtesy of Caprice Vineyards.)

The first commercial vintage of Caprice Vineyards was a 2006 Cabernet Sauvignon made by Dave Palmer of Fiasco Winery. Starting in 2009, Caprice wines have been made at RoxyAnn Winery by John Quinones. Wines offered at the tasting room include estate Chardonnay and Cabernet Sauvignon, as well as a Claret and a Viognier sourced from other vineyards in the area. (Courtesy of Caprice Vineyards.)

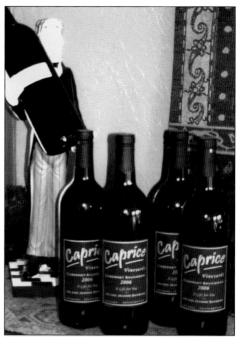

Vineyard owner Jeanne Davidian models an alpaca garment in the company of one of the estate alpacas. The Caprice tasting room provides space for the Davidians' Rolling Hills Alpacas gift shop as well as space for wine. Knitted alpaca products and skeins of yarn from the farm's own alpacas, identified by the name of the animal, are featured. Caprice wines can be sampled inside at a cozy bar or outside on the patio. (Courtesy of Caprice Vineyards.)

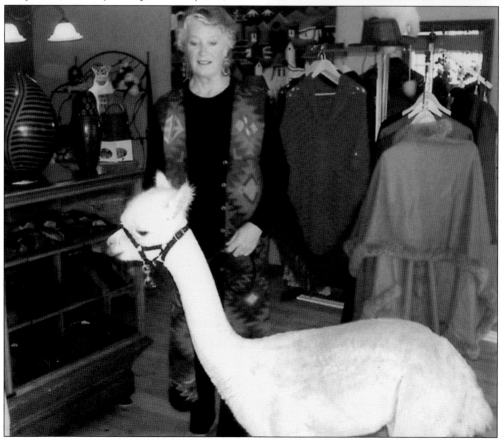

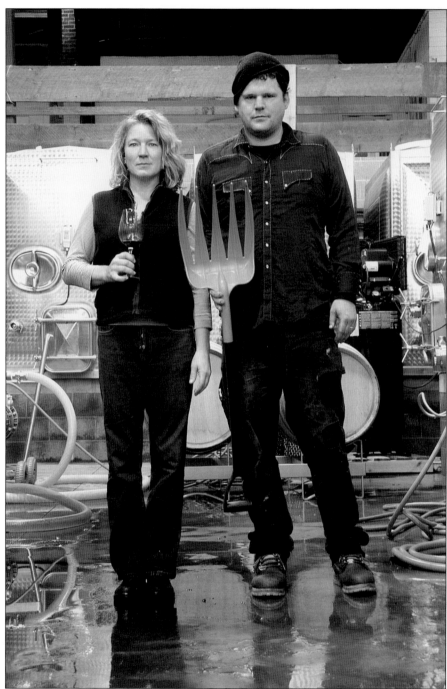

Pallet Wine Company, Southern Oregon's first exclusively custom crush winery, is the brainchild of winemaker Linda Donovan, posing here with cellar manager Patrick Carrico for a "Rogue Valley Gothic" portrait. After 15 years of experience in international winemaking, Donovan established Pallet in 2009 in downtown Medford to provide full-service winemaking, storage, laboratory, wine education, compliance, distribution, marketing, and support services to growers and wineries throughout the Rogue Valley. (Photograph by Teena Jo, courtesy of Pallet Wine Company.)

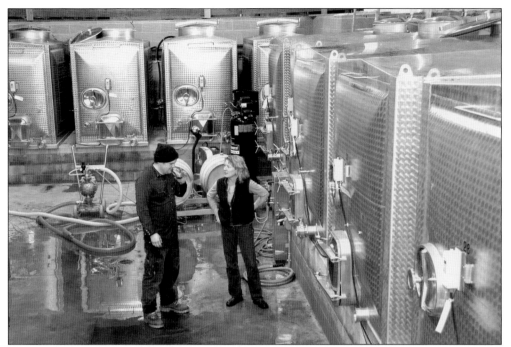

Pallet Wine Company is located in the 21,000-square-foot Cooley-Neff Building, a two-story structure recently added to the National Register of Historic Places. Architect Kenneth Ogden designed the remodel of the building to accommodate a state-of-the-art winery and storage facility, which will handle 20 clients and 300 tons of grapes in 2010. (Photograph by Teena Jo, courtesy of Pallet Wine Company.)

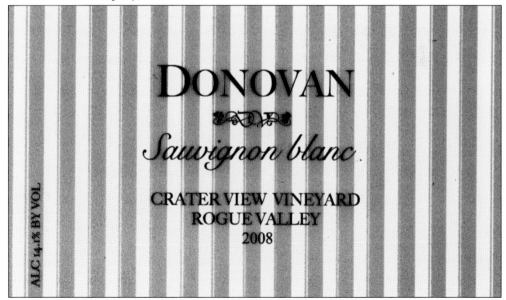

In addition to her custom crush enterprise, Linda Donovan teaches winemaking at OSU Extension and owns the boutique wine brand Donovan. Under the Donovan label, 150 cases of 2008 Mourvèdre and 150 cases of 2008 Sauvignon Blanc were bottled in 2010. Both vintages were sourced from Rogue Valley vineyards. (Courtesy of Pallet Wine Company.)

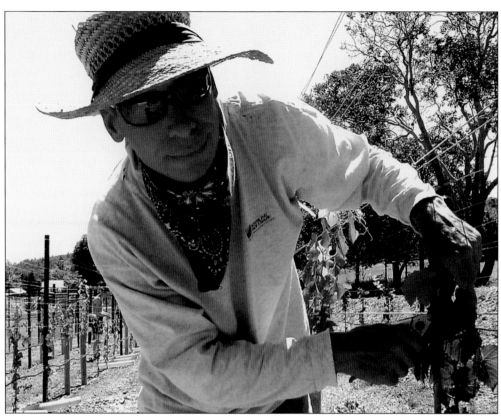

The newest vineyard to be added to the Rogue Valley AVA as of this writing is Dan and Cindy Marca's Dancin Vineyards on South Stage Road outside Jacksonville. The vineyard consists of seven blocks, each analyzed according to soil, microclimate, aspect, and elevation to determine its suitability for a specific clone of Pinot Noir. The first vines were planted in February 2009. Above, Dan Marca trains young vines to the trellis system. Below is the label that will appear on the Marcas' first estate wine, Dancin 2010 Adagio Pinot Noir. (Both, courtesy of Dancin Vineyards.)

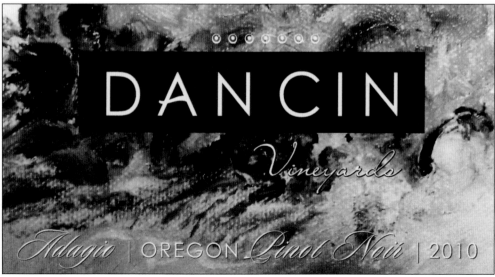

DANCIN

Vineyards

Adagio | OREGON *Pinot Noir* | 2010

Three

INDIVIDUALS WHO HAVE INFLUENCED THE INDUSTRY

The next several pages are devoted to recognizing individuals who have had a distinct influence on the Rogue Valley wine industry. Some have been agricultural pioneers and represent many others whose early efforts to grow grapes in the Rogue Valley eventually paid off. As in the case of grower David Boudry, they are not necessarily part of established commercial ventures but, by virtue of keen personal interest in Rogue Valley growing conditions and product improvement, have become part of the viticultural and winemaking community. Some, such as Sarah Powell, brought international experience to winemaking here and taught others the craft. Others, such as Profs. Porter Lombard and Gregory V. Jones, have had an impact on viticulture not only in the Rogue Valley but in other parts of the world as well. Some, notably Cleve Twitchell and Lorn Razzano, have provided information and education to the public through their newspaper wine columns, fostering a better understanding of the qualities of local vintages. Some, like Ron Stringfield, have used their refined palates to raise the bar in terms of quality, helping growers and winemakers critically evaluate their product. All of these dedicated oenophiles have helped to describe and define Rogue Valley *terroir* and establish the reputation of the Rogue Valley as a wine region.

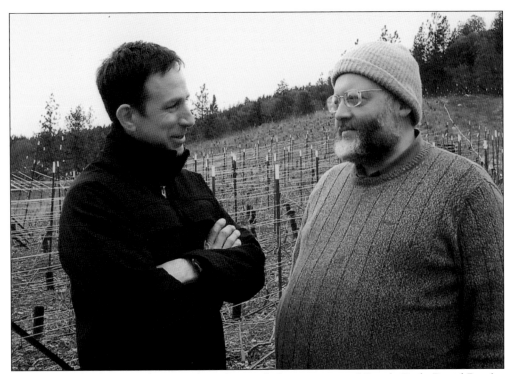

At his vineyard near Antelope Creek in the north drainage area of Grizzly Peak, David Baudry (right) discusses viticulture with Eric Weisinger in 2009. Locating his vineyard at an elevation of 2,600 feet in rocky soil and spacing his vines and rows 1 meter apart, Baudry emulates European viticulture. Recognizing climate and soil characteristics unique to the Rogue Valley, Baudry petitioned the Bureau of Alcohol, Tobacco, and Firearms to create the Rogue Valley AVA. The petition was approved in 1991.

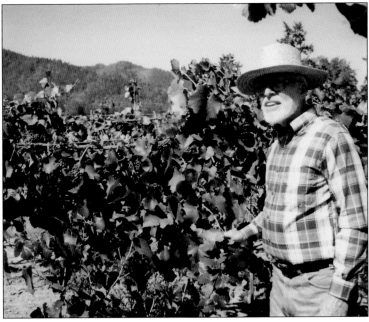

Bernard Smith of The Academy of Wine was the driving force behind the effort to have the Applegate Valley recognized as a distinct American Viticultural Area. He assembled data on the geology, soils, and climate of the area and submitted a petition to the Federal Bureau of Alcohol, Tobacco, and Firearms that was approved in 2000. (Courtesy of The Academy of Wine.)

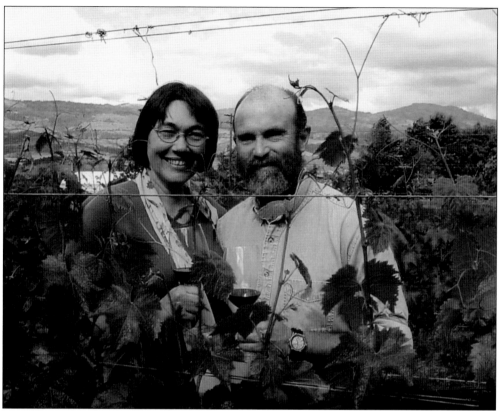

In 1982, after taking a class in viticulture at Rogue Community College, Randy Gold and wife Rebecca bought a pear orchard near Ashland and started Gold Vineyard. He sold his first commercial crop in 1987 and, 13 years later, started Pacific Crest Vineyard Services, the first vineyard consulting company in Southern Oregon. With an expert crew employed exclusively in wine grape cultivation, Gold now manages about 250 vineyard acres and has planted over 500 acres. (Courtesy of Gold Vineyards.)

The late Arnold Kohnert, a pioneer of Rogue Valley viticulture, touted his fruit as "the best Bordeaux grapes in the valley." He established Pompadour Vineyard east of Ashland in 1983, planting 6 acres to Cabernet Sauvignon, Cabernet Franc, Merlot, Malbec, and Semillon. Kohnert kept meticulous records of his vineyard's climate and production, replacing one clone with another to improve quality. Sharing his experience, he strove to improve viticulture in the Rogue Valley. (Courtesy of John Weisinger.)

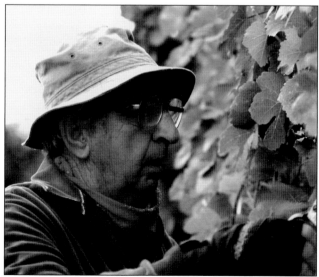

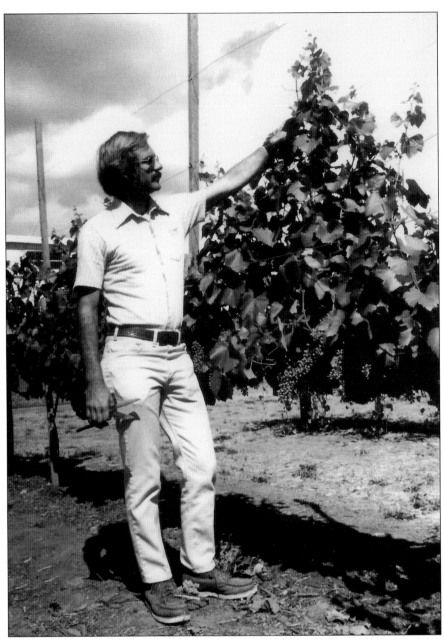

Known as the father of the modern Rogue Valley wine industry, Prof. Porter Lombard, shown in his experimental vineyard in 1973, became the superintendent and horticultural researcher at the OSU Experiment Station on Hanley Road in 1963. Lombard planted the experimental vineyard in 1967, demonstrating that Muscat Blanc, Pinot Noir, Chardonnay, Cabernet Sauvignon, Merlot, and Grenache were viable agricultural options for Rogue Valley farmers. Lombard's pioneering efforts influenced early growers, including John Ousterhout and Dunbar Carpenter, who started their vineyards with cuttings from Lombard's vines. Lombard was instrumental in establishing the International Cool Climate Symposium, first held in 1984. The symposium contributes to the collective understanding of cool climate viticulture and has had a positive influence on the quality of varietals, such as Pinot Noir. (Courtesy of Porter Lombard.)

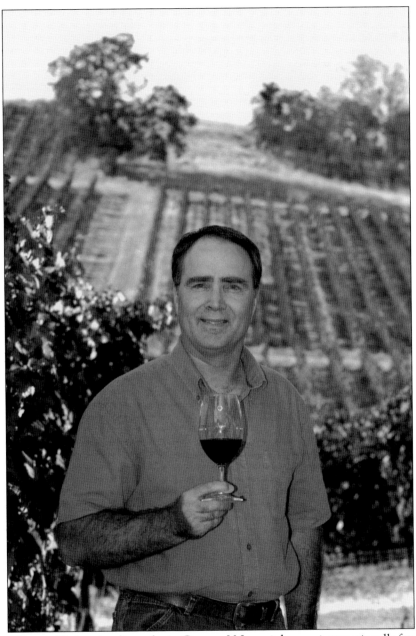

Southern Oregon University climatologist Gregory V. Jones is known internationally for applying the study of climate to viticulture. His research has earned him a global reputation, as demonstrated by his appearance on *Decanter* magazine's "2009 Power List" of the 50 most influential people in the world wine industry. *Oregon Wine Press* named Jones its 2009 Person of the Year, citing his contributions to the establishment of the Southern Oregon AVA, his compilation of data to support planting a greater diversity of varieties in the region, and his readiness to assist growers in selecting the best varieties for their sites. Jones contributed to the International Panel on Climate Change, which scientifically established the connection between human activity and climate change. His studies of viticultural microclimates have been used to define growing regions worldwide. (Photograph by Michael D. Davis, courtesy of Heart to Art—Studio D Photography.)

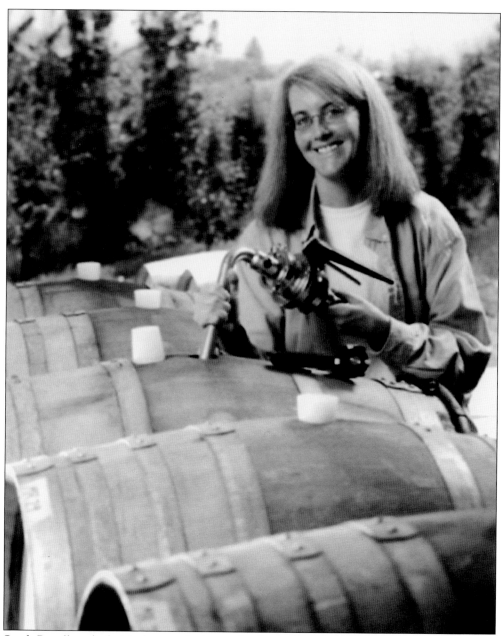

Sarah Powell studied viticulture and wine at the Ecole Agricole in Macon-Davaye, France, and received a degree in Fermentation Science from UC, Davis, in 1988. She made wine in South Africa and at Hogue Cellars in Prosser, Washington, before becoming the winemaker at Foris in 1990. There she established a winemaking style based on fruit cropped at no more than 3 tons to the acre and grown at higher elevations under cool conditions, producing ripeness, richness, and intensity. Foris owner Ted Gerber noted that Powell had "an international palate." After leaving Foris in 2001, Powell established a winery consulting business and became the first winemaker at RoxyAnn Winery. While at RoxyAnn, she established her own label, Sarah Powell Wines. After her death in February 2004, Powell was awarded a Lifetime Achievement Award by the Oregon Grape Growers Association. (Courtesy of RoxyAnn Winery.)

Dr. Willard Brown got his start in commercial winemaking in 2002, assisting winemaker Sarah Powell with the harvest at RoxyAnn, along with Rachel Martin. He completed the certificate program at UC, Davis, in 2006 and was winemaker at Agate Ridge through the harvest of 2007. Brown is known as one of the foremost authorities on the history of winemaking and viticulture in Oregon. (Courtesy of Dr. Willard Brown.)

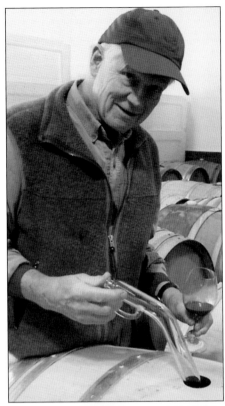

Wine distributor and oenophile Ron Stringfield, shown with friends Nicole Perry (left) and Jody Hupp, held blind tastings for Rogue Valley growers and winemakers from 2002 through 2009. The idea was to have growers taste their barreled wines next to those of their peers and to experience their wines before the winemakers blended them. The blind tastings provided invaluable information freely shared in the spirit of improving the wine quality and the reputation of the appellation. (Photograph by Steve Addington, courtesy of Kiaterna Design Group.)

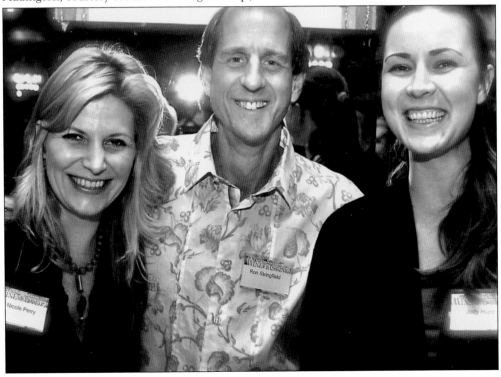

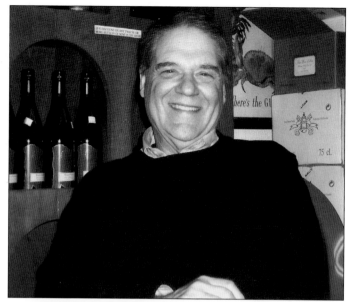

Back when Lithia Way was known as C Street, Lorn Razzano established Ashland Wine Cellar, the oldest wine shop in Oregon and the first to offer over-the-counter tastings. Since setting up shop in Ashland in 1980, Razzano has promoted the wine industry as wine judge, teacher of wine appreciation courses at Southern Oregon University, wine columnist for the *Ashland Daily Tidings*, and originator of the annual Jefferson Public Radio (JPR) wine-tasting fund-raiser.

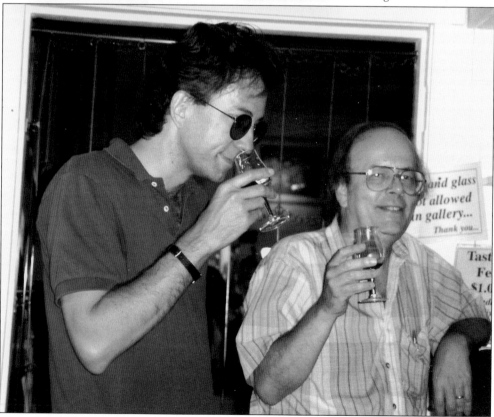

Cleve Twitchell (right), shown tasting wine with son Peter, wrote extensively about Rogue Valley wine while on the staff of the *Mail Tribune* of Medford from 1961 to 2002. Having written over 400 columns to date, he continues as a freelance writer to publicize the rapidly growing Rogue Valley wine scene. (Courtesy of Cleve Twitchell.)

Four

TASTING VENUES
AND EVENTS

There is probably no better way to appreciate the wines of the Rogue Valley than to visit the sites where the grapes are grown and the wines are made. Viewing the terrain and meeting the growers and winemakers can reveal a great deal about the wine before a bottle is ever uncorked. However, if an extended junket to the far reaches of Jackson and Josephine Counties is not on the agenda, there are alternatives. A variety of wine shops, wine bars, tasting rooms, and wine events make sampling Rogue Valley wines a bit less time-consuming and less navigation-intensive. The venues detailed in this chapter were selected for their representation of Rogue Valley vintages, but many also offer excellent food to pair with the wines, as well as staff with a wealth of knowledge of the local wine scene. Many are located in historical buildings that prove interesting in themselves and date back to the 19th century, when Peter Britt first offered his wine for sale at 50¢ a gallon. Occurring throughout the year, the events run the gamut from gatherings held under one roof to a walkabout through Ashland's many fine arts galleries to a ramble by car through the Applegate Valley. Some tasting events represent annual fund-raisers for organizations such as public radio or Science Works Hands-On Museum. The Southern Oregon Winery Association's World of Wine involves professional wine judging. All are aimed at providing the wine consumer with an experience that is highly informative, delicious, and fun.

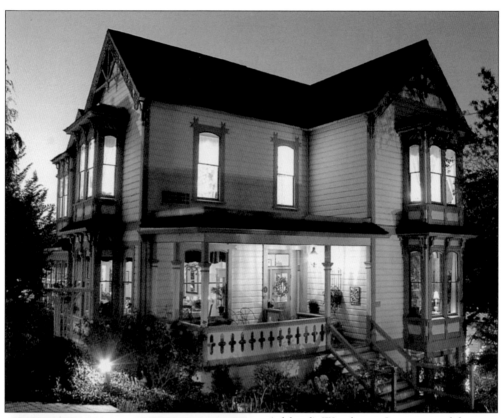

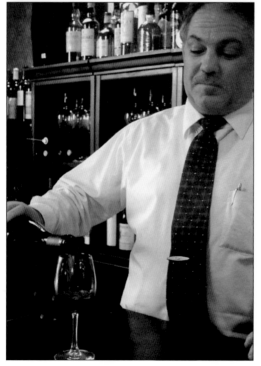

Ashland's Winchester Inn is one of the Rogue Valley's premier destinations for lodging, elegant dining, and wine tasting. Originally the Fordyce-Roper house, the building became a hospital in 1908 and was later moved from Main Street to its present location on Second Street. Laurie and Michael Gibbs renovated the historical building and opened it as an inn in 1982. (Courtesy of the Winchester Inn.)

Winchester wine bar manager Andy Phillips loves to talk wine with visitors and puts together programs of tasting events featuring winemakers and specialists, making the wine bar a destination in its own right. The wine bar opened in 2004 and offers vintages from many Rogue Valley wineries and around the world. It has received the *Wine Spectator* Award of Excellence for three consecutive years through 2008. (Courtesy of the Winchester Inn.)

Special tastings are a daily event at the Winchester. Typical is an evening devoted to Ashlander Paula Sendar's Philanthropie Wine. Philanthropie's Two by Two label, with a dog and cat motif by Ashland graphic artist Jacquelene Ambrose, illustrates Sendar's dedication to animal causes. Philanthropie wines are made by Linda Donovan at Pallet Wine Company in Medford from grapes sourced in the Rogue Valley. Up to 10 percent of profits from wine sales supports animal charities.

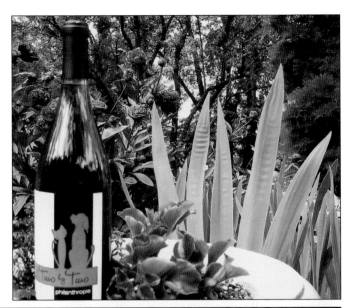

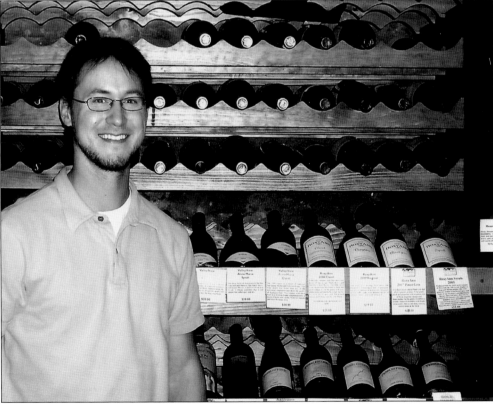

Opened in Ashland in 2000 by Steve and Allyson Holt, the gourmet kitchen store, deli, and retail wine shop known today as Allyson's Kitchen offers paired food and wine tastings every Friday night. Owned since 2009 by partners Lynne Galligan and Jeff Parr, seen here, Allyson's wine shop continues to carry a substantial selection of Rogue Valley Wines in the Southern Oregon section of the cellar.

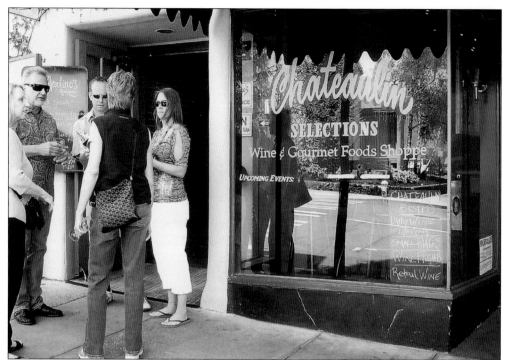

Since 1973, Chateaulin's lace-curtained storefront has graced Ashland's Main Street. The French restaurant had an adjacent wine shop that was replaced in 2010 with a wine bar, above, offering small plates and a wide variety of wines for tasting and retail purchase. The wine selection, shown in part below, includes an array of top Rogue Valley vintages. Under the ownership of Patricia and Doug Volk, the wine bar makeover moves one side of their restaurant in the direction of more casual fare and wine tasting while retaining the original fine dining experience next door.

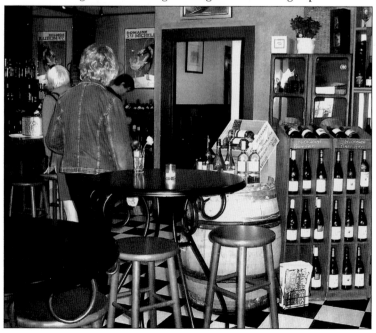

Opened in 2008 on North Main Street in Ashland, Liquid Assets Wine Bar, Restaurant, and Bottle Shop is an excellent place to find Rogue Valley wines amid a worldwide selection. Owners Jim Piotter and Denise Daehler-Piotter have created an informal space with a menu of French-inspired small plates and full dinner entrees, along with a wine list featuring over 20 wines by the glass.

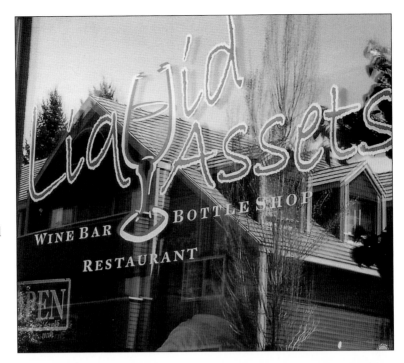

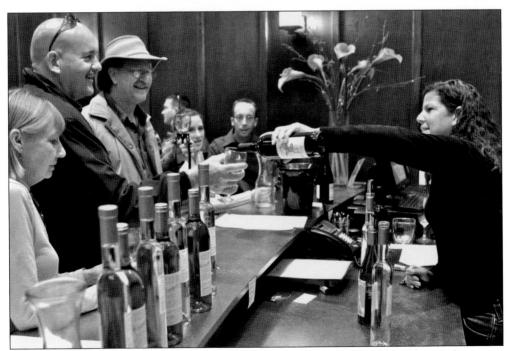

On the Plaza in Ashland next to the Masonic Walkway is Enoteca, Eden Vale Winery's downtown tasting room. Here manager Misty Santos pours a variety of Eden Vale vintages and custom crush labels made at Eden Vale. The name, Latin for "wine library," reflects the cozy interior and the wide variety of wines in the Eden Vale collection. (Photograph by Steve Addington, courtesy of Kiaterna Design Group.)

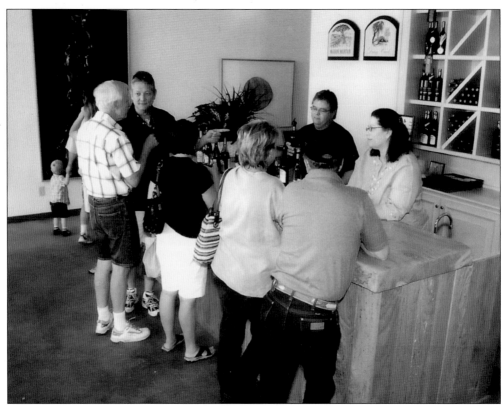

In 2008, Don Mixon and Bret Gilmore of Madrone Mountain joined Russ and Margaret Lyon of Daisy Creek in transforming a 1930s-era three-bay garage (note garage doors still visible below) into a tasting room. Located in Central Point between the Rogue Creamery and the Lille Belle Farms chocolate factory, the Artisan Tasting Room offers visitors handcrafted table and dessert wines paired with world-renowned cheeses and confections. Above, Mixon presides over a busy tasting room with assistant Karen Bkrich. (Both, courtesy of Madrone Mountain.)

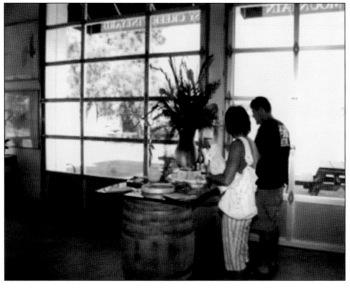

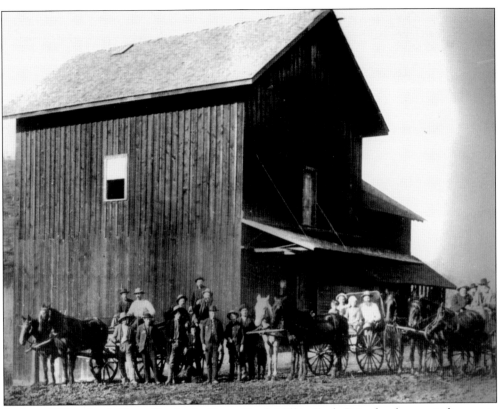

Built in 1872 on Little Butte Creek, the Butte Creek Mill in Eagle Point has been grinding grain with the original belts, pulleys, and stones for over 134 years. Shown here in 1883, the mill was built from trees over 100 years old by pioneers with double-bitted axes and handsaws. Beams were mortised together and secured with hardwood pegs, the details still visible today. (SOHS #2488, courtesy of Southern Oregon Historical Society.)

Owned and operated since 2005 by Bob and Debbie Russell, the Butte Creek Mill provides a variety of stone-ground grain products, as well as an excellent venue for wine tasting in its cellar. Bob Denman pours his Slagle Creek vintages at Butte Creek Mill's Fifth Annual Vintage Fair held in May 2010. He is joined by Mandy Valencia, who offers a selection of Rogue Creamery cheese samples.

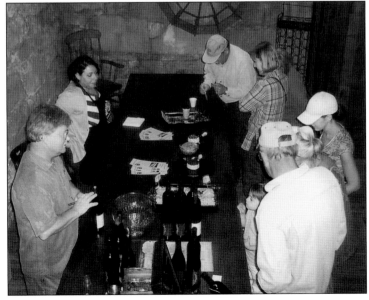

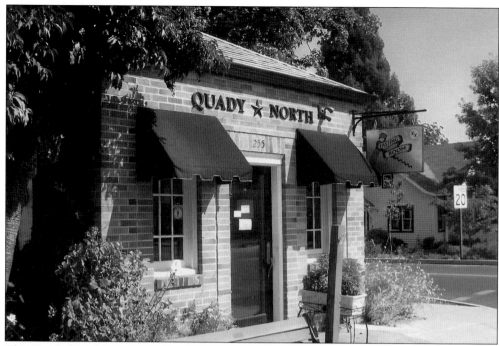

The Quady North tasting room, above, located on California Street in Jacksonville, opened in April 2009. The tasting room features Herb Quady's red and white table wines, as well as the premium dessert wines produced by his father, Andrew, in Central California. Winemaker Herb Quady, below (right), is often on hand at the Quady North tasting room to talk to visitors about his wines—and there's a lot to talk about. Quady North was mentioned as one of the 10 emerging Oregon producers in the February 2010 *Wine Spectator* article "The Cutting Edge." The 2006 flagship Syrah was named a "Stellar Selection" by *Northwest Palate* and received 93 points and Editor's Choice in *Wine Enthusiast*. The 2007 Viognier from Steelhead Run Vineyard received 90 points from *Wine Spectator* and 91 points from *Wine Enthusiast*. (Both, courtesy of Quady North.)

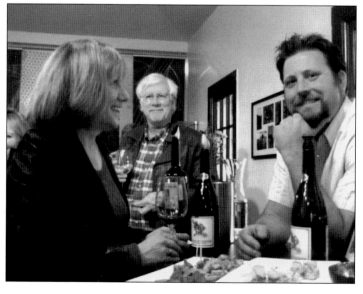

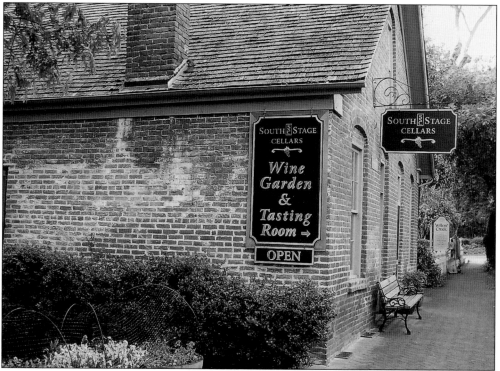

The 1865 brick building in Jacksonville that houses the South Stage Cellars tasting room has been many things: a saloon, doctor's office, butcher shop, and the home of Robbie Collins, founder of the National Trust, which promotes preservation of historical places throughout the United States. The South Stage tasting room showcases wines made from the Rogue Valley grapes of Don and Traute Moore, including the South Stage label, Griffin Creek, Spangler, Dobbes Family Estate, and many others—25 labels in all.

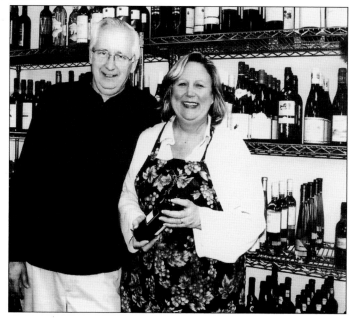

Ken Green and Victoria Guantonio are pictured with a fraction of the wine inventory available for public tasting at their Pacific Wine Club, located near the airport in Medford. Besides the tasting room, there is a 750-bottle fine wine shop and a 1,200-bottle warehouse. The Pacific Wine Club features Rogue Valley wines, such as Cowhorn, Del Rio, Daisy Creek, Eden Vale, RoxyAnn, Slagle Creek, Schmidt, Troon, and Velocity. (Courtesy of Pacific Wine Club.)

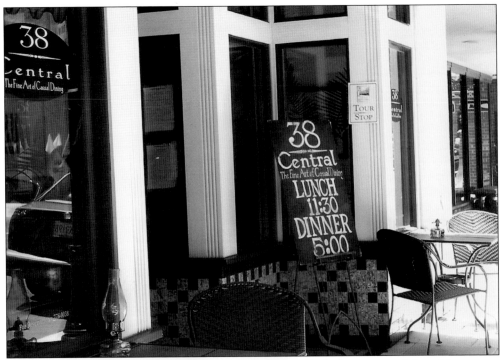

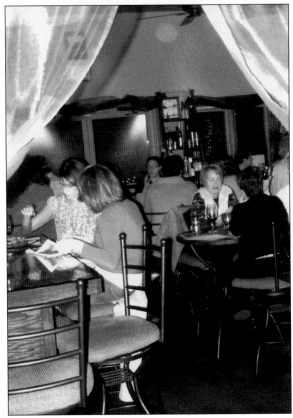

Both the name and the address of David Graham and Michael Kim Wolf's downtown Medford eatery is 38 on Central. After a $3-million renovation of the 1910 Cuthbert Building, the restaurant and wine bar opened in 2008. With its "American Classics" menu, the restaurant offers literally hundreds of wines. On the list are select Rogue Valley labels, including Pebblestone, Cricket Hill, Carpenter Hill, LongSword, Del Rio, Daisy Creek, Troon, RoxyAnn, and Agate Ridge.

A few steps from the Ginger Rogers Craterian Theater in downtown Medford, Corks Wine Bar and Bottle Shoppe focuses on quality boutique wines from around the Pacific Northwest. Rogue Valley wines available include Pebblestone, Daisy Creek, Agate Ridge, Paschal, and Cuckoo's Nest. In addition to a small plates menu, Corks offers a monthly Third Friday Art Walk and Blind Tasting. (Courtesy of Corks Wine Bar and Bottle Shop.)

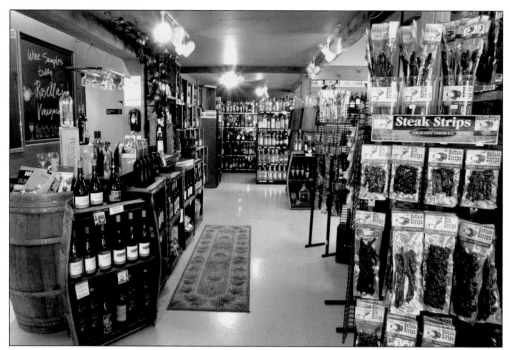

Purveyor of artisan meats since 1966, Gary West Meats is famous for handmade smoked beef jerky, but the store on North Fifth Street in Jacksonville also showcases a wide selection of Oregon wines, including over a dozen Rogue Valley labels. The store features frequent tastings. On this occasion, Rosella's Vineyard is offering samples. (Photograph by Image This Photography, courtesy of Gary West Meats.)

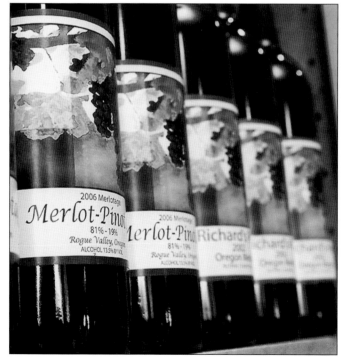

Rising Sun is an internationally distributed purveyor of artisan organic foods with its own wine label. The tasting room on South Pacific Highway in Phoenix offers cheese products and sauces paired with Rising Sun wines by Joe Dobbes of Dundee, Oregon. Pictured is Rising Sun's blend of estate Merlot and Pinotage, a grape similar to Syrah and sourced from Quail Run Vineyards. (Photograph by Mandy Valencia, courtesy of Rising Sun Farms.)

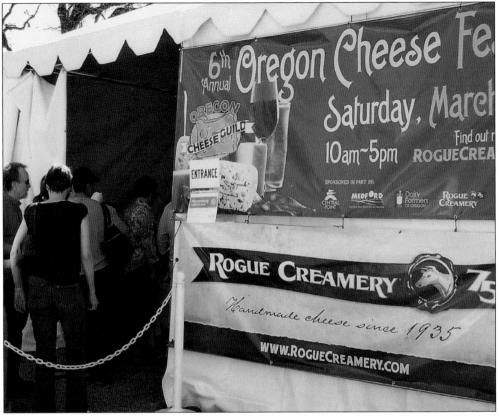

The Annual Oregon Cheese Festival takes place in March in Central Point a few steps from the world renowned Rogue Creamery. In 2010, the festival provided attendees the opportunity to sample wines from 13 different Rogue Valley wineries. The one-day annual event features classes, activities, and live music with wine and cheese tasting.

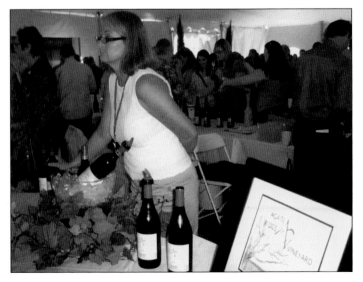

Inside the Cheese Festival tent, Gaylynn Dunagan pours Agate Ridge vintages. Rising Sun Farms, Cowhorn, Cuckoo's Nest, Valley View, Pallet, RoxyAnn, Cliff Creek, Devitt, Del Rio, Slagle Creek, Trium, and LongSword also offered samples of their wines.

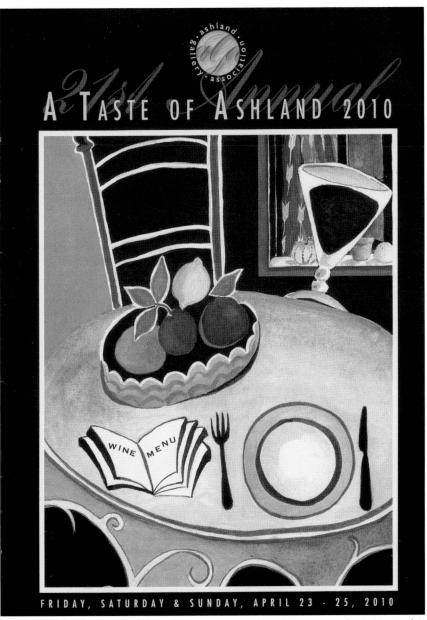

This poster by Ashland artist Katharine Gracey appeared on the program for A Taste of Ashland in 2010. The annual event put on by the Ashland Gallery Association combines a walking gallery tour along Ashland's Main Street and through the railroad district with paired wine and food tasting in the interest of promoting visual arts in the community. With restaurants, caterers, cheese artisans, wineries, distilleries, and breweries offering samples of their wares in participating galleries, A Taste of Ashland is a feast for the senses. The event, staged in late April, kicks off Ashland's tourist season in festive style. Ashland's 30-plus galleries and dozens of artists benefit from the fund-raiser all year long. The Ashland Gallery Association also hosts an art walk on the first Friday of each month, allowing the public to meet artists, view demonstrations, and enjoy traditional and innovative works of art in a gallery atmosphere that often includes music and, perhaps, a local vintage. (Courtesy of Ashland Gallery Association.)

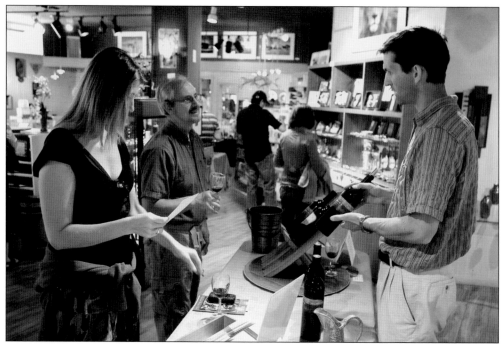

During A Taste of Ashland, winemaker Gus Janeway pours his private label, Velocity, surrounded by an eclectic collection of art objects at Nimbus, an apparel and gift store. Velocity is a velvety red based on Malbec, blended with other Bordeaux varietals, and spiced with a small percentage of Syrah. Janeway has produced about 1,000 cases each year since 2002. (Photograph by Steve Addington, courtesy of Kiaterna Design Group.)

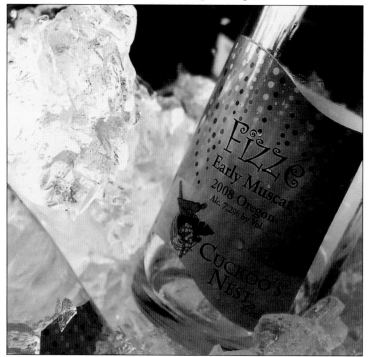

Another proprietary label, Cuckoo's Nest, is the creation of Bryan Wilson, winemaker at Foris. Wilson says the name expresses the fun and lighthearted side of wine. His Early Muscat, dubbed Fizzé, is a sparkling aperitif wine that is made to be iced. At Etienne Gallery, Wilson served a refreshing Fizzé shooter, 2 ounces of Fizzé and a melon ball in a shot glass. (Photograph by Steve Addington, courtesy of Kiaterna Design Group.)

This Science of Wine postcard announces the annual fund-raiser for Ashland's ScienceWorks Hands-On Museum. The three-day event held in May consists of Vine Dining, a five-course dinner showcasing several Rogue Valley wines at the Ashland Springs Hotel, lectures and tastings at the museum, and a red carpet gala with 15 wineries and paired food from local restaurants. (Courtesy of ScienceWorks Hands-On Museum.)

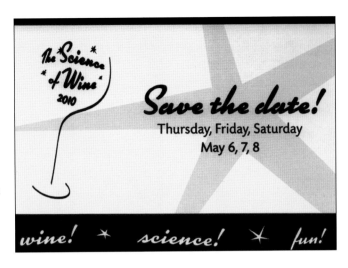

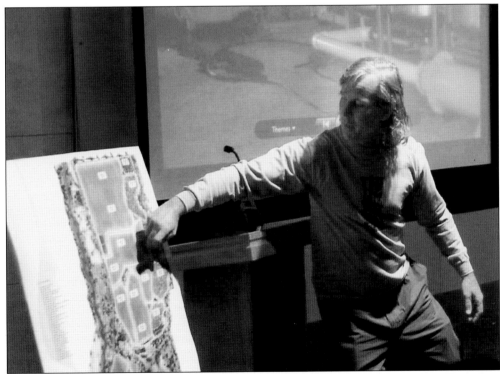

As part of the Science of Wine weekend, Bill Steele of Cowhorn Vineyards presents a lecture on making biodynamic wine. He stands next to a poster of his property showing different vineyard blocks. The vineyard blocks were determined by soil analysis, drainage characteristics, and aspect and have been planted with the specific Rhone variety best suited to each area. (Photograph by Orville Hector, courtesy of ScienceWorks Hands-On Museum.)

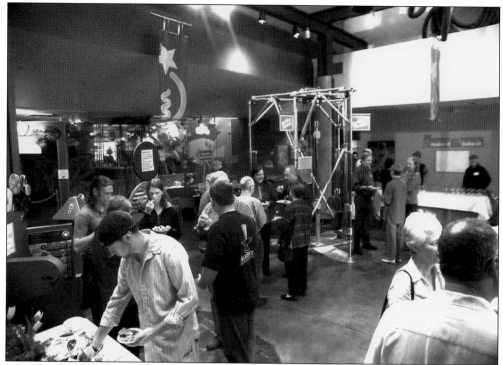

Part of the fun of the Science of Wine is the opportunity to cruise the colorful displays at ScienceWorks. The exhibits are interactive and designed to teach children basic scientific concepts through direct experience. The nonprofit museum funds science education and outreach in nine different countries. (Photograph by Orville Hector, courtesy of ScienceWorks Hands-On Museum.)

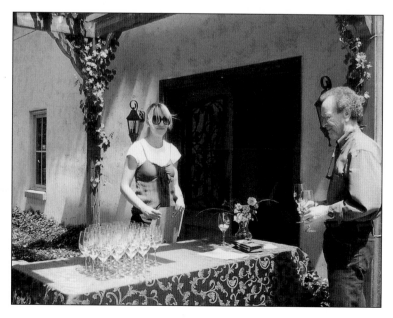

In May and November of each year, Applegate winemakers open their tasting rooms and cellars for a full day of tasting and talking about their wines. Part road rally and part wine tasting, the event, dubbed Applegate Uncorked, begins at Troon Vineyard, where Ashleigh Tamblin (left) provides participant Gary Greksouk with a commemorative wineglass and map.

Troon Vineyard tasting room manager Corey McTaggart (left) pours 1 of over 20 tasting room selections for wine aficionados Jim and Sandi Wester. Troon is 1 of the 14 wineries in the spectacular Applegate Valley that welcome visitors into their cellars for barrel and bottle tastings during the Applegate Uncorked Tour. The tour features delicious appetizer pairings matched with the best wines from each estate. (Courtesy of Troon Vineyard.)

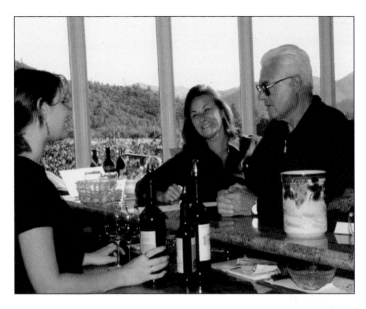

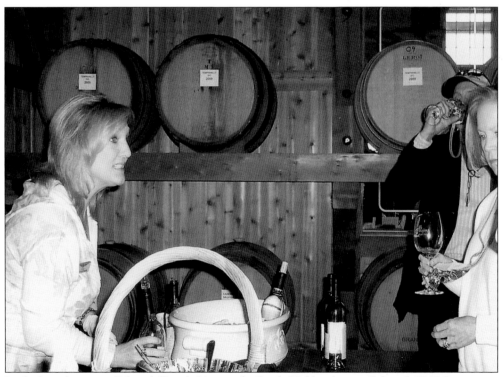

In the barrel room at Schmidt Family Vineyards, Cindy Hubbard pours Schmidt 2009 Sauvignon Blanc and serves seafood mousse on crispy wontons during the May 2010 Applegate Uncorked Tour. On the other side of the barrel room (out of frame), owner and winemaker Cal Schmidt thiefs Zinfandel from a barrel and provides tastes to visitors.

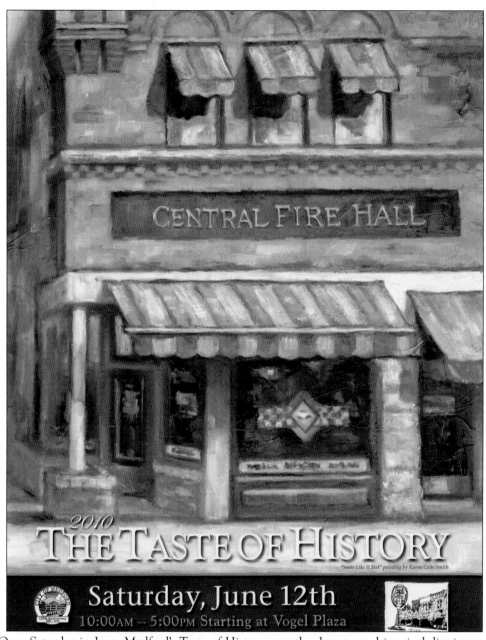

CENTRAL FIRE HALL

"Some Like It Hot" painting by Karen Cain-Smith

2010
THE TASTE OF HISTORY

Saturday, June 12th
10:00AM – 5:00PM Starting at Vogel Plaza

On a Saturday in June, Medford's Taste of History uses the downtown historical district as a setting for a one-day celebration of wine and food tasting, music, and folklore. Visitors may join guided walking tours (one a survey of the architecture of historical buildings and the other a lighthearted crawl of haunted brothels and opium dens) or stroll a variety of downtown tour sites on their own, equipped with wine glasses, of course. There were 17 Rogue Valley wineries on hand for the 2010 event, along with 19 food providers. During the event, the sidewalks of downtown Medford were dotted with poster-sized images of historical structures as they looked when first built, offering a fascinating comparison to the present space. The poster image for the 2010 Taste of History is Karen Cain-Smith's painting of the brick Central Fire Hall, which opened in 1908. (Courtesy of Passey Advertising, Inc.)

The sign at right marks the starting point for the Taste of History in Medford's downtown Vogel Plaza. The plaza is at the heart of Oldtown and adjacent to the site of one of the city's first businesses, George H. Haskins's drugstore, which opened in 1884, the year after the town plat had been recorded. The town was constructed after landowners gave the Southern Pacific Railroad half of the 160-acre site in exchange for locating a depot there. Below, a display shows an earlier view of the 1947 Acme Hardware building in front of the structure today. (Both photographs by Laurie Passey, courtesy of Passey Advertising, Inc.)

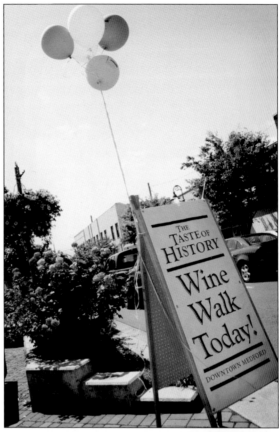

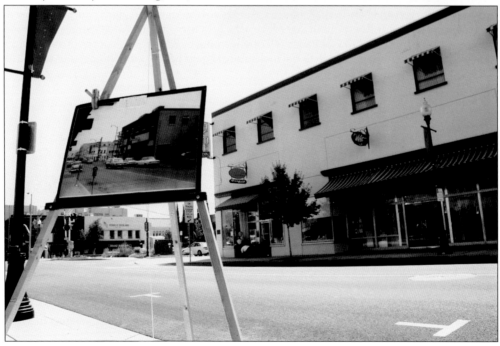

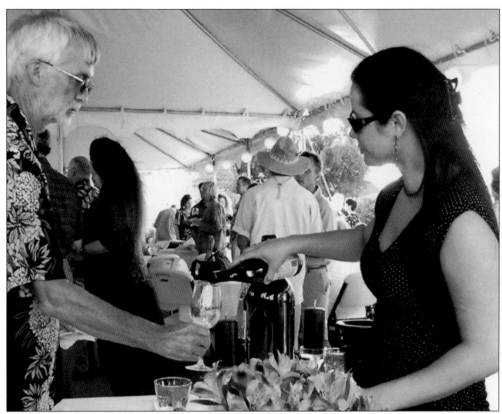

Since 2008, the Klamath Bird Observatory has held its Wings and Wine Gala, a fund-raiser that supports conservation and education efforts on behalf of birds in the Klamath-Siskiyou Bioregion of Southern Oregon and Northern California. Above, Ashlei Michaels (right) pours for a guest at the wine tasting held at RoxyAnn in 2009. The gala, held in September, also features an auction of bird-themed artwork. Below is one such offering, a bronze by Klamath Falls artist Stefan Savides displayed at Eden Vale Winery, where the inaugural gala was held. (Both photographs by Annie Kilby, courtesy of Klamath Bird Observatory.)

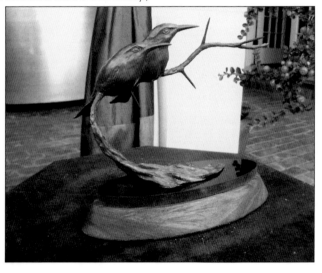

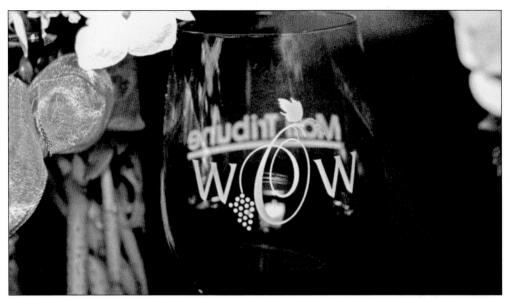

Sponsored by area businesses, the Southern Oregon Winery Association, and the Rogue Valley Winegrowers Association, the annual World of Wine Festival takes place in August at Del Rio Winery in Gold Hill. The highlight of the event is a professionally judged wine competition in which over 40 Southern Oregon wineries participate. Above is the commemorative festival wineglass with the World of Wine logo. Below is one of the 2008 silver medal winners, Rocky Knoll's 2005 Claret. Four out of five 2008 gold medalists were Rogue Valley entrants (Carpenter Hill 2006 Petite Sirah, Foris 2006 Pinot Noir, Paschal 2004 Syrah, and Velocity 2005 Velocity), as was the Best of Show (Cliff Creek 2004 Claret). (Both photographs by Teena Jo, courtesy of World of Wine.)

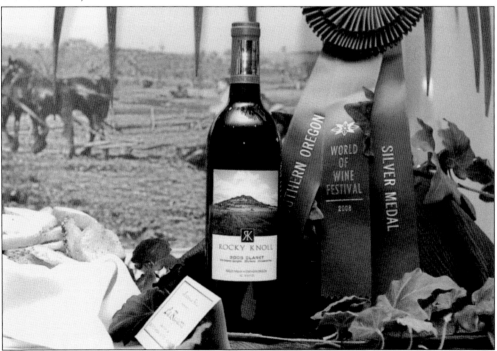

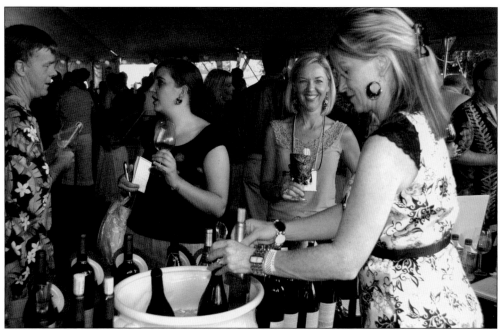

A wine that garnered praise at the 2009 World of Wine Festival was Viognier. While many experts feel that the Rogue Valley has the potential to produce excellent Rhone varietals, Viognier had not generated much buzz until 2009, when entries in the tasting competition outnumbered Syrahs. A thick-skinned grape that can handle heat, the variety has begun to gain traction in the Rogue Valley over the past decade. Above, Nancy Iannios pours a variety of Schmidt Family vintages, including the 2008 Viognier that took a silver medal in the 2009 competition. Below, World of Wine attendees stroll the silent auction tables. (Both photographs by Teena Jo, courtesy of World of Wine.)

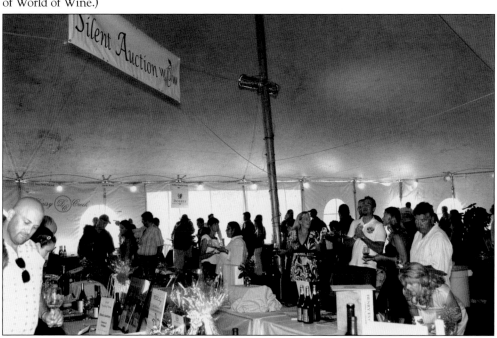

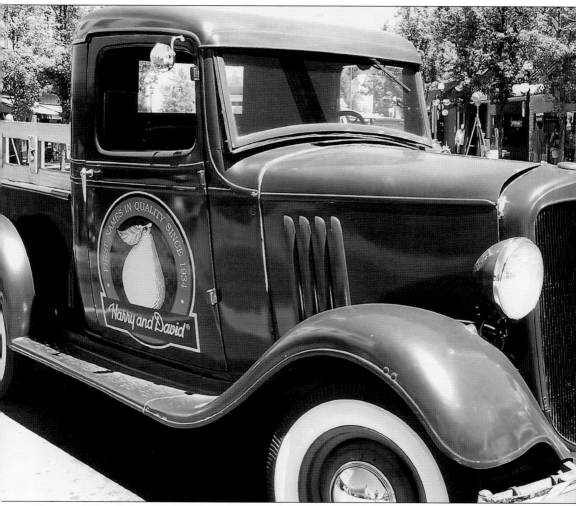

Harry and David, America's premier direct marketer of fruit and food gifts, began in 1910 when Seattle hotelier Samuel Rosenberg purchased 240 acres of pear orchards in Medford. Today the multimillion-dollar purveyor of specialty food lines, known especially for its "Fruit-of-the-Month-Club," is still headquartered in Medford. The Harry and David vintage truck is a symbol of the fruit business then and now. The Harry and David Country Store in Medford provides locals an alternative to mail-order shopping. In September, the store puts on A Taste of Harry and David, an annual event featuring live music, over 50 food sampling stations, and wine tasting by many Rogue Valley wineries. The two-day event draws 3,000 people.

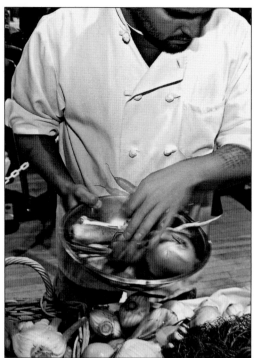

In November, the Ashland Chamber of Commerce sponsors the Southern Oregon Food and Wine Classic. The three-day event showcases the bountiful harvest of Southern Oregon vineyards and the farm-to-table concept. Beginning with a Friday evening wine reception, the weekend includes food preparation and wine education workshops and a Chef Showdown competition. Here, chef Franco Console of Omar's Restaurant of Ashland chooses vegetables for his entry in the culinary competition. (Courtesy of Ashland Chamber of Commerce.)

Highlighting Ashland's annual Southern Oregon Food and Wine Classic are a variety of Rogue Valley wines. Liz Wan of Troon Vineyard is on hand to offer tastes of popular vintages, including Druid's Fluid and River Guide White. (Courtesy of Ashland Chamber of Commerce.)

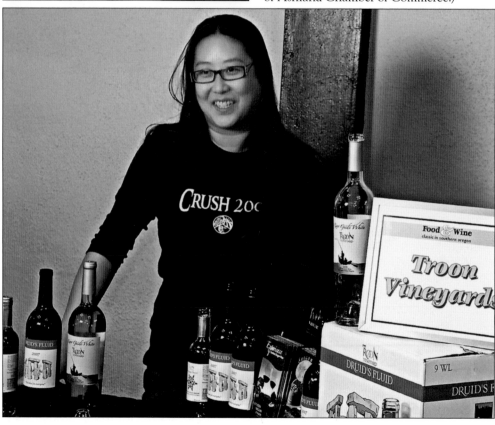

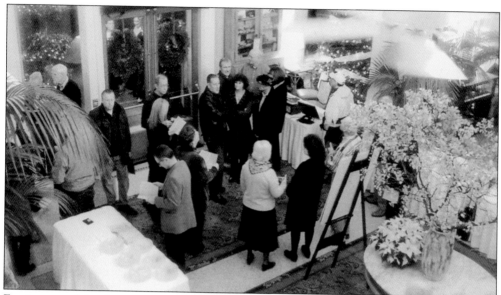

For its annual fund-raising event in December, public radio's JPR taps the yuletide spirit of oenophiles with a wine tasting and silent auction held at the sumptuous Ashland Springs Hotel in downtown Ashland. Above, JPR supporters are shown arriving in the lobby of the hotel, a Main Street landmark built in 1925 and originally named the Lithia Springs Hotel. At nine stories, the hotel was the tallest building between San Francisco and Portland at the time it was built. Renamed the Marc Antony in 1960, the structure was totally renovated and reopened as the Ashland Springs in 2000. Below, Michael Donovan of RoxyAnn Winery provides holiday smiles and sips of wine.

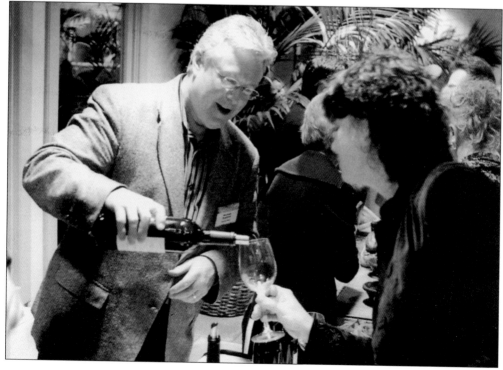

BIBLIOGRAPHY

Follansbee, Joseph G. "Liquor and the Law: Prohibition in Southern Oregon." *Table Rock Sentinel.* May 1988: 4–11.

Hellman, Edward W., ed. *Oregon Viticulture.* Corvallis: Oregon State University Press, 2003.

Jones, Gregory V., and Lea Light. *Site Characteristics of Vineyards in the Rogue and Applegate Valley American Viticultural Areas.* Ashland: Southern Oregon University, 2001.

Love, Roger. "The Rebirth of Oregon's Wine Industry." *Table Rock Sentinel.* May 1988: 12–15.

Miller, Alan Clark. *Photographer of a Frontier; The Photographs of Peter Britt.* Eureka, CA: Interface California Corp., 1976.

Peter Britt: The Man Behind the Camera. Jacksonville: Southern Oregon Historical Society, 2004.

www.nass.usda.gov/or

www.rvwinegrowers.org

INDEX

Academy of Wine, The, 41, 42, 94
Agate Ridge Vineyard, 86–88, 99, 112
Applegate Red Winery, 29
Bear Creek Winery, 19
Bridgeview Vineyards and Winery, 24, 25, 54
Caprice Vineyards, 88, 89
Carpenter Hill Vineyard, 78
Cliff Creek Cellars, 77
Cowhorn Vineyard, 56, 57, 115
Crater Lake Cellars, 80, 81
Cricket Hill Winery, 42, 43
Cuckoo's Nest Cellars, 114
Daisy Creek Vineyard, 73, 106
Dancin Vineyard, 92
Deer Creek Vineyards, 26, 27
Del Rio Vineyards, 75, 76
Devitt Winery, 50
Eden Vale Winery, 78–80, 105
Fiasco Winery, 46, 47
Folin Cellars, 82, 83
Foris Winery and Vineyards, 22, 23, 98
Granite Peak Winery, 75
Grizzly Peak Winery, 74, 75
John Michael Champagne Cellar, 35, 36
LongSword Vineyard, 40

Madrone Mountain Vineyard, 51, 52, 106
Pallet Wine Company, 90, 91
Paschal Winery and Vineyard, 70
Pebblestone Cellars, 71, 72
Philanthropie Wine, 103
Plaisance Ranch, 44, 45
Quady North, 55, 108
Red Lily Vineyard, 53
Rocky Knoll Vineyard, 64, 65
Rosella's Vineyard, 39
RoxyAnn Winery, 84–86, 99, 125
Schmidt Family Vineyards, 48, 49, 117, 122
Siskiyou Vineyards, 20, 21
Slagle Creek Vineyard, 38, 107
Soloro Vineyards, 57, 58
South Stage Cellars, 66, 109
Trium, 67–69
Troon Vineyard, 33, 34, 116, 117, 124
Valley View Winery, 30–32
Velocity Cellars, 114
Weisinger's of Ashland, 60–63
Windridge Vineyards, 28
Wooldridge Creek Vineyard and Winery, 36, 37

www.arcadiapublishing.com

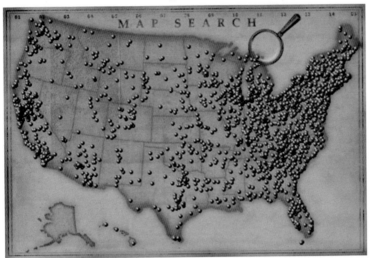

Discover books about the town where you grew up, the cities where your friends and families live, the town where your parents met, or even that retirement spot you've been dreaming about. Our Web site provides history lovers with exclusive deals, advanced notification about new titles, e-mail alerts of author events, and much more.

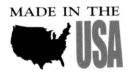

MADE IN THE USA

Arcadia Publishing, the leading local history publisher in the United States, is committed to making history accessible and meaningful through publishing books that celebrate and preserve the heritage of America's people and places. Consistent with our mission to preserve history on a local level, this book was printed in South Carolina on American-made paper and manufactured entirely in the United States.

This book carries the accredited Forest Stewardship Council (FSC) label and is printed on 100 percent FSC-certified paper. Products carrying the FSC label are independently certified to assure consumers that they come from forests that are managed to meet the social, economic, and ecological needs of present and future generations.

FSC
Mixed Sources
Product group from well-managed
forests and other controlled sources

Cert no. SW-COC-001530
www.fsc.org
© 1996 Forest Stewardship Council

Find Your Place in History.